PEARL BUCK'S

LIVING LEGACY

The Welcome House Story

by Dale Yoder

PEARL BUCK'S LIVING LEGACY
THE WELCOME HOUSE STORY

Copyright © 1999
by
Dale Yoder
206 Neversink Road
Reading, PA 19606

Second Edition, 2008

Library of Congress Number: 99-740249
International Standard Book Number: 978-1-883294-85-4

Reprinted 2008 by
Masthof Press
219 Mill Road
Morgantown, PA 19543

CONTENTS

DEDICATION

This book is dedicated

to my parents,

my brothers and sisters,

and all others

who have made

Welcome House

a loving success.

I hope many learn from their example.

PREFACE TO THE SECOND EDITION

For many years, I resisted writing the story of our Welcome House family. While I felt it was an experience that should be preserved for posterity, I was concerned that my constant presence in the events of our life might be interpreted as a disguised attempt at an autobiography.

However, when I discovered that many in our community had little knowledge of what Welcome House was ("part of Welcome Wagon," "a home for delinquents," "I never heard of it") I put aside my reluctance and decided to proceed. It had become clear to me, the dedication of our parents and the multitude that supported Welcome House deserved to be remembered accurately. This was my motivation. Encouraged by family and friends, I began the history which became a true "labor of love."

The original printing of *The Welcome House Story* has helped to achieve my goal. Two thousand books are now in circulation. Also, since the publication, I have lectured or discussed the book on fifty-five occasions to groups ranging from church congregations of 400 or more to small book clubs of a dozen. Undoubtedly, thousands have learned the meaningful, loving story of Welcome House. In response to the book I have received dozens of letters commenting on the amazing commitment of our parents and others to come to the aid of children in need— letters from as far away as Florida, South Dakota, Utah, Ohio, and Indiana. The local response has been likewise overwhelming, and I don't consider this a response to me, but to the truly uplifting example of our parents and their lives. With this second printing the message continues.

The second printing is the same as the first, with a few minor corrections. However, a number of important details need to be mentioned. Pearl Buck International, with Welcome House as its adoption arm, continues to work its miracles. Some new people have been added. Janet L. Mintzer is the president and CEO. Under her guidance, the organization has had growing success. Over 10,000 adoptions have now taken place. Also, the organization's support of international children is growing. In a world filled with strife, innocent victims need relief. Pearl Buck International provides this service. Though Asia has been the targeted area for the organization's help, plans are currently underway to expand into other parts of the world. What remarkable growth since the day in 1948, when a little East Indian child was brought to the door of Pearl Buck because he had no place to go. The single home she began, our Welcome House Family, was the seed that has grown to help thousands and thousands. This is one of Pearl Buck's many legacies. And in a delightful indication of the circle of life, David, the first Welcome House child, is now a hard-working, contributing member of the Pearl Buck International Board of Trustees.

Dale Yoder
2008

PREFACE

The year was 1948. The place was Blooming Glen, a little village in the center of Bucks County, Pennsylvania. There, the typical small-town family of Lloyd and Viola Yoder, schoolteacher and store clerk respectively, was about to undergo a drastic change. From two children—Charlotte, sixteen, and myself, twelve—the family would grow to twelve children during the next four years. This was not a miracle of biology, but a miracle of love. Ten Asiatic-American brothers and sisters joined the Yoders through these years, forming what was to be called Welcome House. This successful international family reminded a land that vigorously resisted racial integration that it could be achieved. And this new and very different family was just the beginning.

After our international family was formed, successive actions followed that helped to alter the racial make-up of America. Though Welcome House was intended as an immediate solution to the virtual homelessness of the ten Asiatic Americans who were to become my brothers and sisters, evidence suggests that a much larger social phenomenon followed.

For instance, beginning in the early 1950s and influenced by our family's example, adopting children of Asian heritage became an acceptable American practice. In those years, Welcome House was the principal means for this change. The Welcome House Charter, originally allowing foster-home placement, was altered to include an adoption option. Over the next four decades, thousands of children were adopted through Welcome House.

Pearl Buck, the central figure in this movement, later organized a second foundation called the Pearl S. Buck Foundation. Its primary goal was to provide food, clothing, medical supplies, and shelter for Asian-American children abandoned and ostracized in East Asia after the Korean and Vietnam conflicts ended. In this case, over 25,000 were helped. In addition to these specific services of the two foundations, Welcome House officials advised other adoption agencies in the expanding and fruitful area of Asian placement, further increasing the number of Asian-Americans placed in loving homes. By these actions, many Americans demonstrated a new attitude toward Asians, which was a remarkable shift from earlier prejudiced ways—immigrant-exclusion laws, vicious acts of discrimination, "dirty Jap" assessments of World War II, widespread belief in "yellow race" inferiority, and the like. It would be self-serving and ludicrous to claim that all these changes are a direct result of the original Welcome House, but is undeniable that Welcome House was born in a time when its intended goal was unpopular, and conventional wisdom and actions among the American people resisted such "race mixing." The history of the time would suggest that Welcome House was a beginning. And, as the Chinese philosopher said, "A journey of a thousand miles begins with the first step." This is the story of one such journey.

This remarkable, innovative accomplishment was the result of the love and nurturing of my parents; the wisdom and generosity of Pearl Buck and her husband, Richard Walsh; the advice and contributions of the board members that Pearl Buck recruited; the generosity of the many people who donated time and funds; and the constant support of friends, community, church, and school. It was a joyous time. As one who was there when it unfolded, I share these moments of an unusual life experience from my memory, from the available written record, from the comments of my brothers and sisters, and from the insights of friends and relatives who were so vital to its success.

The same people who helped Welcome House succeed are many of the same people who were so important in bringing these memories to print. I hesitate to name them because I know some very significant people will be overlooked. Those who were specifically interviewed are cited in the text as well. With apologies to those omitted, I acknowledge the following:

- from the Pearl Buck family, Jean Walsh Lipponcott and Janice Walsh gave me important details of the Walsh perspective during the days and weeks when Welcome House was forming.

- Margaret Fischer, an original Welcome House board member, was particularly insightful about the early discussions that created the Welcome House organization and those that shaped the Welcome House adoption process.

- Edward Beister, son of one of the early organizers, also provided informative details about the early years from the perspective of his parents and his own memories.

- particular friends of the family like Elvin and Pattie Souder, Wally and Helen Shaddinger, Charles and Maggie Hollenbach shared memories and relived many meaningful moments of those days.

- Helen Shaddinger was Pearl Buck's private secretary for many years, and she and Pearl Buck's chauffeur, Frank Ottenger, were very valuable sources of information.

- Ellis Graber, pastor of Zion Mennonite Church of Souderton during the fifties, returned from his retirement in the West to participate in Zion's 100th Anniversary in 1989, and documented the influence that Zion and the parishioners had on our family as the children grew.

- John Grasse, superintendent of the Hilltown Schools, and William Keim, superintendent of the Pennridge consolidation, were important leaders who represented the many ways the school supported the Welcome House family.

• Olive Solliday, elementary schoolteacher and close friend, remembered the years when the Welcome House children were in her class.

• Kathleen Bayer, a current Welcome House administrator, and Grace Sum, past executive director of the Pearl Buck Foundation, provided important history and statistics of the two foundations which have now united into a single organization, an appropriate step in the struggle to aid Asian children in America and in other parts of the world.

From the beginning, our many friends have been immeasurably important—the Ralph Moyers, the Hilton Spanningers, the Al Parisis, the Herbert Stauffers, the Len Iles, the Harold Clymers, and on and on. From each of these families comes childhood friends of mine as well: Jim and Brooke Moyer, Leon Iles, Jim Clymer, Jack Spanninger, and Vince Parisi. Through the years continued conversations about the old days in Blooming Glen, the impact of my dad on their lives, our athletic moments, or what-have-you, have found their way into the pages that follow.

My brothers and sisters must also be acknowledged: Charlotte, now Mrs. Charles Strouse; Sumi, now Mrs. Craig Gerhardt; and Lillian, now Mrs. Charles Walton, are the distaff siblings. The Yoder brothers include Frank, Ray, Bob, Scott, Dave, Leon, and Paul. Jack was killed in a tragic car accident almost thirty years ago. Each knows how important Welcome House has been to their well-being; likewise, each knows how important we have been to each other; each has contributed to these pages, first by living it and then by discussing it.

I must also acknowledge and thank a number of people who have helped me with the completion of this study. Being a member of a college faculty has given me the opportunity to seek the advice and expertise of others in the college community. William Hummel, James Reppert, Jeffrey Woodward, and James Moyer of the Albright College faculty have read all, or portions, of this text and have offered helpful advice. Barbara Fahy, John Pankratz, and Michael Adams have been especially insightful with written suggestions, including some structural revisions and editorial corrections. However, as is always the case, responsibility for errors in fact, logic, or presentation rest solely with me. Michael Miller, a past Albright history major and now a graduate student at the University of Florida, was invaluable in providing some technical needs, from proofreading to Xeroxing. I also give special thanks to three very able and forgiving typists: Diane Gattone, Bunnie Druzba, and Peggy Reiniger. Also, my sincere thanks to Masthof Press, for without Lois Ann Mast and her staff, all this work would have been for naught.

Finally, my loving thanks to my wife Nicole. She has contributed to every stage of this work; without her encouragement, this study would still be in the planning stage.

Bibliographic Explanation

Pearl Buck's Living Legacy; The Welcome House Story is a story based on local memory. The basic outline for the story comes from my own recollections as I lived through these early years of Welcome House (1948 to 1957). Next, family and friends add details and validate the accuracy of the outline. In addition, local written records provide more information with some memory validation as well, i.e. Welcome House board minutes; *Green Hills News*, a summer newspaper written and printed by Pearl Buck's children, later aided by Welcome House children; promotional pamphlets of Welcome House, rich in details and statistics; letters of Pearl Buck and others. Also, Pearl Buck's writings frequently mentioned the Welcome House experience, with many references to the life and times of the unusual family. *Life* magazine and other news accounts further documented life at Welcome House in popular and frequent fashion. All of the collected memories and documents were spun into the happy tale of love and devotion that the Welcome House experience was.

The local story of Welcome House is placed within the context of the times and, hopefully, this makes the study more than a family album of anecdotes and traditions. From this perspective, the story can be seen as a significant social action, a truly successful example of minority assimilation during a time when many resisted such actions.

In order to achieve this end, the national experience is presented during the years of Welcome House growth and vice versa. Documentation for the national record is as follows.

1. Much of the general history of the twentieth century that is discussed falls into the category of common knowledge and is included in the study with that understanding.
2. History of discrimination against Asian-Americans:
    Stanford M. Lyman, *Chinese Americans*, Random House, 1974.
    William Petersen, *Japanese Americans*, Random House, 1971.
    Ronald Takaki, *Strangers From A Different Shore*, Little Brown, 1989.
3. The conceptual information about the "Second Reconstruction":
    C. Vann Woodward, *The Strange Career of Jim Crow*, Oxford, 1966.
4. The concept of irrational actions in politics and minority life:
    Richard Hofstadter, *The Paranoid Style in American Politics, and Other Essays*, University of Chicago, 1965.
5. Books by or about Pearl Buck:
    Pearl Buck, *My Several Worlds*, John Day Publishers, 1954.
    Pearl Buck, *For Spacious Skies*, John Day Publishers, 1966.
    Pearl Buck, *Letter From Peking*, John Day Publishers, 1957.

Peter Conn, *Pearl S. Buck: A Cultural Biography*, Cambridge Press, 1996.

Theodore Harris, *Pearl S. Buck: A Biography*, John Day Publishers, 1969.

Beverly Rizzon, *Pearl S. Buck: The Final Chapter*, ETC Publications, 1989.

Warren Sherk, *Pearl S. Buck: Good Earth Mother*, 1990.

Nora Stirling, *Pearl S. Buck: A Woman in Conflict*, New Century, 1983.

6. Books about the forties and fifties:

Joseph Goulden, *The Best Years: 1945-1959*, Atheneum, 1976.

David Halberstam, *The Fifties*, Fawcett Columbine, 1993.

Daniel Horowitz (ed.), *American Social Classes in the 1950s*, Bedford, 1995.

J. Ronald Oakley, *God's Country: America in the Fifties*, Dembner, 1986.

Cabell Phillips, *Decade of Triumph and Trouble: The 1940s*, MacMillan, 1975.

7. Books about adoption:

Pearl Buck, *Children For Adoption*, John Day Publisher, 1963.

8. Concept of cultural pluralism and diversity:

Arthur Schlesinger, Jr., *The Disunity of America*, Norton, 1995.

These are the sources that document *Pearl Buck's Living Legacy; The Welcome House Story.* One final note—for this study, I have chosen the example of others who, in combining a historical analysis with a personal story, have omitted footnotes to facilitate the flow of the story. Where necessary, I have included the reference in the text.

- Dale Yoder

INTRODUCTION

This is a story of love and devotion—a story that glories in the traditions that promote America's virtues. Though America often fails tests of virtue, perhaps some will find herein examples of truth and love that do persist at the core of American life. American institutions are vitalized here—family, religion, education—and the love story told should rally many to believe that America has a sense of justice and equality—blurred though it may often be.

The love story is not one of the boy-meets-girl variety. Rather, it concerns the love that flamed in the hearts of one Pennsylvania family in the years after World War II—a family that grew in size because circumstances demanded that a social injustice be met head on.

I tell this story with mixed feelings. On one hand, I feel very strongly that it deserves to be told, and I find a great deal of interest whenever I share some details with others. However, since I am a constant presence throughout, I fear it might be interpreted by some as a disguised attempt at autobiography. But truly, I was only an incidental participant and observer. Family and friends have urged me to proceed and so I do. The real heroes are my parents, Pearl Buck, and the multitudes that rallied around a remarkable pioneering social experiment. In brief, Pearl Buck created an Asiatic-American family, the Welcome House family, made necessary by the unfortunate presence of racism and its demeaning effect on the lives of people whose only fault was to be born with the wrong color skin.

The story begins in the winter of 1948. Pearl Buck, the Nobel Prize-winning author of *The Good Earth* and other successful books about East Asia, faced a tragic dilemma. A New York adoption agency had an unwanted dark-skinned East Indian-American child with no place to go.

Knowing of her interest in East Asia, the agency came to her. "What can we do?" the agency officials asked. "The child cannot be placed." Seeing an innocent child rejected by both East and West, since neither American nor East Indian families wanted the mixed-blood toddler, Pearl Buck responded quickly and compassionately. She took the child and fulfilled his needs by forming a family around him. My mother and father were recruited as the parents of this unwanted one-year-old.

During the next four years, our family added nine more Asian-American children who became a lively, loving household, albeit an unusual one. Our parents with their dozen children (the ten plus my sister and myself) made quite a different family than the earlier, more traditional family of Frank B. Gilbreth, made famous by the book, *Cheaper by the Dozen*. Understandably, we heard that phrase many times over the years as we were frequently compared to that publicized family, particularly after Clifton Webb starred in the movie of the same name, made in 1950. Such comparison usually produced a smile or two. We knew we were very different from the other dozen—different in origin and in composition. But we also knew we were something special. And through love and cooperation, we fashioned our own family traditions and memories. Now all my brothers and sisters have gone on and established families of their own; but without exception, we continue to share the love and togetherness begun so many years ago. Our traditions continue and our memories live on.

Welcome House began as a spontaneous response to a particular need. Though it was not a grand design for restructuring American life, its significance must be understood. The family was a local example of the nation's changing pattern of race and ethnic relations that was unfolding in this country during the post World War II years. These racial and ethnic changes were long overdue. Throughout our history, isolated voices reminded us of the wrongs of slavery, anti-Semitism, Native American genocide, and the like, but too few listened. The circumstances of World War II got our attention, however. The atrocious racism of Adolph Hitler was too vivid and too excessive to disregard. The inhumanity of such violence caused many Americans to take stock of our unfair racist practices and heed the call for reform. So in these years after World War II, America seriously questioned and began to alter its racial and ethnic configurations. Welcome House was one local component of this make-over attempt, a microcosm in the macrocosm of social change.

What follows is an attempt to combine my personal experience with my profession—teaching recent American history at Albright College, a small liberal arts school in Reading, Pennsylvania. I recognize the danger of attempting to serve both ends. Yet, I feel that the human interest qualities of the "Welcome House story" add a specific component to the changing ways of a post-war world.

Naturally, there are many family anecdotes, but there is also the presence of larger social history that amplifies the new ways of life, be it television technology and all its manifestations, school consolidation and the end of the little red schoolhouse, or a new world order with an emerging East-West division that frightened us all. Welcome House grew in this age, and in times of frustration and failure, a story with a happy ending is a joy to cherish. Qualified persons will judge the professional merits of this work, but I hope all who read it will agree that my parents should be remembered as caring and loving people who in their own, virtually innocent way made a difference, and that our family, so unnatural in make-up, will be viewed as a natural family in practice.

— *Chapter 1* —

THE NATIONAL SETTING:
A GLIMPSE OF AMERICAN LIFE
DURING THE EARLY YEARS OF
WELCOME HOUSE

Welcome House was born in 1948, an age with a "best of times/worst of times" complex. For some, the promise of American life was fulfilled. Success bred confidence and the future seemed unlimited. As Norman Mailor's hero in *The Naked and the Dead* states so matter of factly, "The spirit of the world is ours for the taking." But there was a dark side to this life as well. For too many, the American Dream fell short. Poverty, discrimination, and the consequences could not be eradicated by denial or optimistic recounting of the "good times." Such problems had to be addressed, directly and energetically, if they were to end. Within the euphoria of the times, there was a planned attack on such problems, thus acknowledging their existence. But no one knew as the post-war years began who would support such a plan or what the outcome might be.

On the surface of American life at this time, celebration was most evident, for we had much to celebrate. Even those with little or nothing rallied 'round, for most believed the American Dream would reach them eventually. Besides, some things affected all Americans. For instance, the big war had recently ended and made us the greatest power on earth. Our wealth and our power seemed unending.

The American scene was an opening cornucopia of riches and plentiful bounty. Economically, our gross national product jumped from $212.3 billion in 1945 to $286.2 billion in 1950, touching the heart and soul of the country with new houses, new cars, new gadgets. We had been able to make the world a safe place for democracy through our military power, now we would make it a better place through our technology. All would benefit from our leadership and innovation. It was the American Dream in action. Work hard; take advantage of opportunities; good things will naturally follow. There was no stopping us. Such was the conventional wisdom.

The optimist said these were "the best years of our lives," and an Oscar-winning movie proclaimed this in title and in sentiment. The film told the story of an injured war veteran who returned home and overcame his disability to marry his high school sweetheart and "live happily ever after." But the movie was, in fact, a repository of the dichotomous times. The public, for the most part, overlooked another veteran in the movie who returned to an unhappy marriage, found love in a tumultuous affair, and ended up divorced and out of town. Nevertheless, the movie was viewed as proof that these were the "best years of our lives." American optimism in the land of opportunity overwhelmed any negative reminders. The public interpreted this as fiction mirroring life, and they loved it.

A popular World War II song proclaimed that "when the lights go on again all over the world, there would be time for things like wedding rings, and sweethearts would sing." Now that the lights were on, the country was delirious. The age reflected the message in a multitude of ways. Books, movies, magazines, radio, and the new rage, television, regaled their audiences with the wonders of the American dream. Popular culture, its instruments everywhere pervasive, bolstered the country's sense of our own abilities and future prospects. There was no stopping us. This was conventional wisdom in action.

Noteworthy evidence of the American dream was the experience of Harry S. Truman. In 1948, he won a brilliantly conceived upset victory for the Presidency over the projected winner, Governor Tom Dewey of New York. Here, too, was a message. A man of the people had prevailed, so the system must work. Only in America could such a record be forged. At age thirty-seven, Truman had a failed business, no college training, and few prospects. Within two decades, he became the leader of the mightiest nation on earth. Only in America. What a great country. This, too, was the conventional wisdom.

But were these American dream images an accurate measure of the times? How would poverty be reduced? What was the effect of racism and sexism? Was Hubert Humphrey's impassioned defense of Civil Rights at the Democratic Convention of 1948 the sign of the times—an indication that minority needs were truly being considered? Or should one emphasize the old values of racism that were represented by Strom Thurmond and his followers who bolted that same convention to form their own segregationist, Dixiecrat Party? Perhaps a better movie symbol of the times is the 1947 Academy Award movie, *Gentlemen's Agreement*. Here virulent anti-Semitism marred the optimistic values of American society. Undoubtedly, the good times were not universal, and this was the underside of American life that needed a thoughtful overhauling.

The principal political leader of the late 1940s, Harry Truman, committed his administration to the overhaul. His "Fair Deal" attacked political and economic inequities, seeking to improve the quality of life for all through government intervention where necessary. His policies included increased minimum wages, workmen protections, and tax reform, among other things. His ideas were not new. Rather, they continued the liberal political and economic evolution of the twentieth-century America.

History tells us of reformers and politicians who questioned the fairness of the capitalists' power at the end of the last century, and demanded new ways to improve America. For the most part, these changes have been associated with liberal political platforms—Progressivism, New Freedom, New Deal. Truman extended these liberal programs with his Fair Deal. Later, the New Frontier and the Great Society would add to this tradition. The century-long struggle resulted in widely accepted economic and political changes, such as voting rights for women, safety standards for the work place, child labor laws, urban sanitation controls, and conservation of natural resources. The list could be expanded. Even though liberalism has lost some of its glamour in the present day, few could deny the efficacy of such reforms as they improved American life.

Minority rights are glaringly absent from this list, though changes were sorely needed. As recently as World War II, legalized segregation for African Americans, Native American reservations with sub-standard living conditions, Japanese-Americans in concentration camps, blatant anti-Semitism and lingering anti-Catholicism were normal patterns of American life, all too widely accepted.

Harry Truman, though a seemingly unlikely protagonist for minority rights, launched an attack on discrimination and intolerance as part of the broad text of the Fair Deal. He seemed miscast in this role because, according to some historians, he was a racist. They felt the atomic bombing of Japan exposed his racism toward Asians; also, in the 1930s, as a new congressman in Washington, he displayed a blatant anti-black bias, undoubtedly the product of his Missouri background where his granddad once owned slaves.

Others held a different opinion. For them the atomic bombing was a war measure against an enemy, not against another race. Furthermore, his later public statements were fair-minded and generous, not vicious and racist. He spoke of the need to help all people. Reports of black soldiers being beaten and harassed on their return from World War II disturbed and moved him greatly. His bias of an earlier time was muted. With new-found convictions, he used his power to make things better for minorities. His presidential decree to integrate the armed forces was the first shot fired in the war on discrimination in this post-war period. The national movement to redress the crimes of racism and intolerance would continue through the next fifty years.

Historian C. Vann Woodward called this reform effort America's Second Reconstruction, a time when changing laws for minorities reminded him of post-Civil War Reconstruction. In that first period, the legal system eliminated slavery and tried to foster ways to bring the "Freedmen," as the ex-slaves were called, into mainstream America. But unfortunately, Reconstruction failed, sadly replaced by a disastrous system of segregation. It took more than a half century for powerful figures to mount an attack on that court-supported, but immoral segregation, an attack that was shaped in the twenty-five years after World War II, but in reality continues right down to today.

The Second Reconstruction reached all levels of American life. Federal government actions were the core of the movement. Presidential decrees, Supreme Court decisions, and Congressional mandates resulted in the integration of the Armed Forces (Truman, 1948), the end of the "separate but equal" principle (Brown Supreme Court decision, 1954), and the creation of a Civil Rights commission (Congressional action, 1957). Through these and other measures, the government took a firm stance against discriminatory ways. Consequently, Jackie Robinson led a multitude of black stars into major league sports; school integration was put in motion; federal officers protected the civil rights of minorities; eventually housing and occupational discrimination carried federal penalties; film and television began to highlight minority stars; minority political figures emerged to lead the struggle for justice.

The changes were impressive, but the struggle was not over. Racism still was an ugly presence. Substandard housing on Native American reservations, racist groups with white superiority claims, exploitation of Mexican-American migrants, educational and income differences for blacks and whites—these were just some of the measurable and identifiable conditions that remained.

One particularly tragic example of violent, irrational reaction to changing racial patterns was the murder of a black Chicago youth in Money, Mississippi, during the summer of 1954. Fourteen-year-old Emmitt Till, visiting his grandfather, violated a social convention of the South when he spoke fresh to a white woman. For saying "bye Baby" to a store clerk as he departed a local grocery, he was beaten, shot to death, and thrown into the Money River. His known killers, the husband and brother-in-law of the young clerk, were acquitted of the crime. We know their role because later they sold their story to a magazine. In their confession, they bragged that they did it because the country had to be saved from such brashness and the over-all drift toward integration.

Hooded Klansmen North and South, White Citizen Councils, American Nazi Party—these were formal groups that said no to attempts of civil justice for all. Without question, racist emotions were evident and rampant. Any observer could see that the civil rights movement was not greeted by all with bell ringing and hosannas. In fact, if one considers the strong emotion that produced police dogs, cattle prods, Lester Maddox, George Wallace, the Ku Klux Klan assassinations, bus burnings, ad infinitum, it takes no genius to conclude that denying the American dream to the masses was a popular pastime and any self-congratulation for our progress was questionable. We still had a long way to go.

This was the racism that existed as Welcome House was forming. Could this type of hate be directed toward an innocent family with Asian-American children? And what was the racists' feeling toward Asian-Americans in general, both past and present? Such information would be additional clues in assessing the way Americans would react to Welcome House.

The history of Asian-Americans is not encouraging. It began in the middle of the nineteenth century with the Chinese. They came in the 1860s to perform what has been described as "coolie labor" for the transcontinental rail-roads. The Chinese were used for particularly hazardous tasks in traversing the Rocky Mountains, tasks that were deemed too dangerous for white men. Discrimination continued for the Chinese throughout the rest of the nineteenth century and this intolerance was institutionalized by the incredible Chinese Exclusion Act passed by the United States government in 1882. The law specifically excluded Chinese laborers from our shores and refused citizenship to all Chinese. The Act was a horrible example of racism and further indication of the expanding belief in an "inferior yellow race."

Japanese fared little better. Due to the exclusion of Chinese immigrants, Japanese were recruited for the "coolie jobs." From 1885 to 1924 Japanese came in large numbers (196,543). But after 1924, federal quota laws effectively halted all Asian immigration. Before the quota laws, the Japanese were well received since they filled unwanted jobs. Eventually, when they proved to be very willing and able workers, American attitudes changed. They were perceived as a competitive threat to the American work force, and resentment developed. First, labor unionists physically attacked Japanese cobblers and coolies in San Francisco in the 1890s. Later the infamous San Francisco School Board Act of 1906 segregated the city's Japanese students, prompting a Japanese Imperial Government protest.

Hoping to avoid an international incident, President Theodore Roosevelt intervened and overrode the School Board's order. But harmony did not become the norm. When Japanese workers turned to farming and quickly succeeded, more white opposition formed. Various discriminatory actions were set in motion. States passed laws to control alien land-owning. Barber shops, restaurants, and other public places excluded the Japanese. Employment was offered only for undesirable tasks. Furthermore, virtually all social contacts were denied. With ease and in apparent good conscience, the same irrational judgments and actions previously directed at the Chinese were now repeated against another Asian people.

This racial and ethnic attitude continued into the twentieth century. Many examples illustrate this. A popular book with a sad message gave pseudo-intellectual credence to the notions of racial and ethnic inferiority. Madison Grant, in *The Passing of a Great Race* (1916), wrote of American fear that the Great White Race would be mongrelized by invading ethnic and racial hordes. He called for White Anglo-Saxon leaders to act forcefully to save our civilization. Grant's call did not fall upon deaf ears. Many believed his words. Even the United States government, at least partially influenced by Grant, implemented a quota on immigration. The series of acts passed in the 1920s ended the "immigrant-invasion." Immigration fell from the millions to the hundreds, and in the minds of racists, our civilization was saved.

Of course, World War II intensified our anti-Asian feelings. The "dirty Jap" became a household phrase. Franklin Roosevelt's executive order incarcerating over 100,000 Japanese-Americans was the ultimate act of irrational fear. These were Japanese-Americans who were distinguished members of their respective communities, mainly in California. Many had sent their sons to do valiant battle in Italy against the Axis foes. Even so, they were herded into southwestern concentration camps and, without due process, stripped of their homes, their possessions, and their dignity.

Only recently has the U.S. government admitted its error in this action and paid minimal reparations to the Japanese families. This historic trail of discrimination and intolerance carried into post-war America. It was an unholy tradition, and it left Asian-Americans with a second-class citizen status not unlike African-Americans or Native Americans.

Past hostile discrimination against Asians and the vigorous attack on the Second Reconstruction by certain racist groups offered a grim forecast of what might befall Welcome House. The national mood did not seem very receptive to an integrated family. Yet, amazingly, during the years of the emerging Second Reconstruction, Welcome House grew and prospered. By contrast to the national effort that met such vicious resistance in many places, Welcome House took shape without incident. This remarkable difference begs for an explanation. Why were the vociferous challenges to our national reform not forthcoming in the community around Welcome House?

The answer to that question is the principal focus of this study as I relate the Welcome House story. The success of Welcome House for the children that were saved from a life of discriminatory despair is a joy for the participants. The success of Welcome House as an example of what love, commitment, and community support can do to confront a sorry social condition is a message that touches the hearts of all who hear it, and hopefully becomes a useful plan to attack other social injustices. Enthusiastic cooperation, prideful boasting about "their" Welcome House, material support—these were the ways that the local community greeted Welcome House. What a difference from cattle prods and public demonstrations. Why? Part of the answer is clear and logical. Ten little children, and however many might later follow, do not constitute the kind of threat that the national bigot had identified when he saw school integration, blacks in government, blacks in professional sports, or high wages for migrant workers.

Still, it must be remembered that these children were unwanted non-persons before Welcome House; other small groups of "different" types have historically met with strong resistance. Witness the Shakers, the Black Muslims, the strong feelings expressed against local communes during the 1960s, the destructive attack on Move members in Philadelphia, and more recently, the carnage in Waco, Texas.

Undoubtedly, small groups have had significant actions directed at them. Thus, the absence of any sort of racist reaction toward the Welcome House family requires some deeper analysis. Briefly, it seems the local institutions were successful. Church, school, family, and community sensed the needs of Welcome House. Each offered a variety of ways to support and sustain the family, and each will be examined in detail. The result is a revealing contrast between the national and the local levels, for the two are very clearly different. Considering the happy results, one can't help recalling the rhetoric of the American Dream, and see the reality of it unfolding in the happy experience of ten unwanted children who grew and prospered in family love and community acceptance during those years of national trauma.

So in summary, these were the conditions that existed during the early years of Welcome House. We were a nation with a tragic history of racism directed at African-Americans, Native Americans, Asian-Americans, and others; a nation with an awakened conscience that was attempting to remedy our past wrongs; a nation with many individuals maintaining old racist values and resisting, emotionally and violently, the call to redress those past wrongs. The situation was volatile and dangerous and, with supreme irony, these conditions were part of an age when the country had great self-esteem and a widely-held belief that we were the greatest place on earth.

Chapter 2

THE LOCAL SETTING:
THE BUCKS COUNTY ENVIRONMENT
IN THE LATE 1940S

Consider: 1) central Bucks County, a rural locale of Pennsylvania Dutch farmers and virtually all-white villages addressing the long history of Asian discrimination through a remarkable social experiment, an integrated Asian-American family; 2) Blooming Glen, a peaceful, isolated, homogeneous village vigorously supporting such a venture; 3) Lloyd and Viola Yoder, ages forty-one and thirty-nine respectively, happy and secure in their life-style suddenly discovering themselves as parents of this path-finding family; 4) Pearl Buck, a wealthy, internationally-known author becoming grandmother to the new children and providing financial support, friendship, and counsel for a vital, creative solution to a tragic social condition. This was the site and these were the original players in a most uncommon tale of social change. Before it began in 1948, no one could have predicted such a scenario. Truth might truly be stranger than fiction, considering these happenings. But happen they did, and with them began a most wondrous story.

The story unfolds in rural Bucks County because Pearl Buck was here. She was the lightning rod that caused the changing social configuration. She had moved to Bucks County in 1934 after the success of *The Good Earth*. Some might claim that divine intervention must have brought her to this community. Clearly, she preferred rural New York or New England for her country estate. Clearly, the dilapidated farmhouse she found in southeast Pennsylvania was far inferior to homes she inspected in the

North. But her choice was the uninhabited three-bedroom farmhouse with the broken windows, missing shutters, and overgrowth of weeds. Perhaps it's true, she saw the wonderful potential of the fifty-acre farmland—the hillside vista, the swift-moving stream, the remodeling possibilities of the sturdy stone farmhouse.

Perhaps the romantic part of her was captivated by historical legacy, the charm of the community, and the legend of Devil Hen. In her autobiography, *My Several Worlds*, she writes in revealing fashion: "For myself I was pleased to discover that I had bought land belonging once to Richard Penn, William's brother. And it was interesting that twice when we pulled up a vast dead tree, we found coins mingled with its earth, not of great value, but once Spanish coins and again English. I liked the evidence that earlier people had lived here before me."

Somewhat surprisingly, she confirms that she even liked the notion that a former owner, Devil Harry (as she calls him), was still around. Whether walking the fields with Buck's startled gardener or breaking kitchen cups before a frightened maid, Devil Harry was a ghost who stalked the homestead, probably searching for a way to atone for past sins. According to local legend told to me by my father in a fuller account than that recorded in *Several Worlds*, Devil Hen (not Devil Harry, though Henry, Harry, Hen are commonly interchanged) and his long-suffering wife were former owners of the Pearl Buck farm.

Briefly from a tale that is probably apocryphal, and certainly embellished, Devil Hen was a farmer who didn't like to farm. His lazy habits led to failure and poverty and caused much unhappiness for his wife. During one of the Devil's regular afternoon naps, his wife fell victim to the strain and frustration. Though highly illegal, of course, the Devil's wife tied a rope around the neck of the napping farmer, pulled the rope through the open heat vent into the upstairs bedroom, and with the body of her husband dangling below, tied the rope to the bedpost. She then ran screaming and crying to the neighbors shouting, "Come quick! Devil Hen hung himself!" the neighbors rushed back to find Devil Hen sleeping peacefully with the family's potbellied stove hanging from the ceiling. Devil Hen had awakened before the deed was accomplished, removed the rope from his neck, and tied the rope to the potbellied stove. Probably tired from his efforts, he returned to his more important nap, much to the chagrin of his wife. Historical legends, personal ghosts, strong-willed women—all would have been attractive to the fertile mind and imagination of Pearl Buck. So, was it the potential of the farm? Was it the romantic wistfulness of the great author? Or, was there a fateful attraction to the Bucks County area?

For whatever reason, Pearl Buck was in Bucks County, and by the early 1940s had completed the renovations of the broken-down farmhouse. Electricity, running water, bathrooms, a new kitchen, and an office wing made the old farmhouse into a grand country estate called Green Hills Farms. In addition, she had purchased five surrounding farms totaling over 500 acres, and had established a most luxurious, though certainly pastoral life. From this rural fiefdom, with servants, swimming pool, and tennis court, located approximately two miles from the little town of Blooming Glen, Pearl Buck would travel weekly to New York City to take care of her publishing work. With her cosmopolitan lifestyle, her international fame, and her vast wealth, it would seem totally incongruous for a friendship to develop between the family of the Nobel Prize-winning celebrity and the family of a local schoolteacher and athletic coach. But from such improbabilities come some of life's most interesting stories. Here are some of the particulars.

Our original family was small—only my parents, my sister, and myself. We lived in a small house in a small village in eastern Pennsylvania. The village, Blooming Glen, is situated about thirty-five miles north of Philadelphia and twenty miles west of the Delaware River. Although we didn't know it, it was this setting that was to become the site of a most unusual social change—Pearl Buck's creation of a multi-racial family in the heart of an all-white, rural Pennsylvania community.

It is crucial to know something of this setting because the success of Pearl Buck's legacy depended upon acceptance from the community in which it was spawned. Few need to be reminded that somewhere throughout the land in those days were supporters of black segregation in sports, schools, public parks, and swimming pools. Also, there were those who agreed with the Roosevelt administration's order to incarcerate Japanese-American citizens in virtual concentration camps, stripped of their possessions and their dignity. Likewise, many held general attitudes that made "dirty Jap," "drunken Indian," and "lazy nigger" acceptable labels. Was Blooming Glen part of this unholy tradition?

During the 1940s, a map of the community would show two streets crossing at a point where a garage, a grocery store, and a hotel called attention to the hustle and bustle of Blooming Glen life. The town businesses included the garage, two grocery stores, a farm implement shop, a barber shop, a shoemaker, the hotel, a feed mill, a pants factory, and a tinsmith shop. Also, an insurance office, a piano teacher's studio, and a local country doctor's office were service-oriented enterprises. Finally, on opposite edges of the town were a stone quarry, a creamery, and two meat-processing establishments. Surrounding the town were numerous farms, raising table vegetables, wheat and other grain, and milk cows. A population of 300 was sprinkled along the crossroads of Blooming Glen, living in houses that gave little clue to any population differences. True, some houses were larger, but all were well-kept, and none were opulent. An outsider would likely assume that this was a happy, self-contained village with a thriving economic structure and a satisfied population of equals. Such an observation would be correct.

Our family was typical of others in the town. We were part of the rural, white Protestant, Republican America of that age. My father's position as the local high school teacher and coach probably gave us slightly more prestige and slightly less income than the average family in the town. But, in reality, this was a homogeneous society. True, there were economic, religious, and educational differences among the people, but these differences did not produce hostile religious enclaves or sharply defined social or class lines. We were a community.

Economically, the business owners and the butter-and-egg men (local entrepreneurs who took eggs, chickens, fruit, etc., and sold them on established routes throughout the Philadelphia suburbs) seemed to be the most successful. However, there was little observable difference between such individuals and the factory workers who went off to the U.S. Gauge in nearby Sellersville. All worked hard and enjoyed the life their efforts provided. Occupational differences counted little as all gathered each evening at the post office. Mail had to be picked up at the post office and local gossip was shared while waiting for the postman to distribute the mail into each pigeon-hole and give his relieved "all out" call.

Though the town had no borough status with an accompanying town government, there were community activities that helped to blur any differences that occupation might produce. The local baseball diamond was a good example. An association had been formed somewhere in an unrecorded historic past, and the local men enjoyed the camaraderie of grooming the field and deciding what measures should be taken to improve the park. New bleachers and lights for night softball indicated that progressive decisions were being made. The community spirit continued with other projects. In the center of town the men erected an honor roll, listing the names of all community members who served in World War II. Fund raising (cake sales, newspaper collection, town fair) financed educational programs not covered in the regular school budget. And most ambitiously, the community donated time and money to build a small, but functional, gym for school and community use. The women also ran an active Ladies Auxiliary for the Sellersville Hospital, Sewing Circle, and church groups that added to the town's well-being, and helped produce a sense of community. In effect, there was no evidence of a social hierarchy; there was no feeling that anyone was "too good" for any others in the town.

The same sense of community was present in the town's religious life. With Mennonites, Methodists, Lutherans, and Roman Catholics in town, there seemed a potential for religious divisiveness. But tolerance and respect prevailed. In fact, all the religions contributed to a singular religious purpose, leading a moral life that fulfilled the Golden Rule. To illustrate, the town had only one church, an "Old Mennonite" congregation. About half of the townspeople and a large percentage of the nearby farmers belonged to this church. Their religion taught belief in pacifism, adult baptism, and a simple lifestyle. Members were economically successful (both grocers, feed mill owner, many butter-and-egg men) and active in the community affairs discussed above. Their plain clothes (prayer caps and bonnets for women, no ties for men) made little difference to others in the community. The rest of the town belonged to Protestant churches in nearby places.

Our family was part of a liberal Mennonite branch frequently referred to as "New Mennonites." As might be expected, the more conservative Mennonites, by contrast, were identified as "Old Mennonites." Our General Conference, though committed to the basic tenets of pacifism and adult baptism, had rejected the Old Mennonites' controls on everyday life. Dress style, church architecture, certain church service conventions, and use of all modern technology are a few of the basic distinctions. Our church, Zion Mennonite, was in Souderton, about eight miles west of Blooming Glen.

The only exception to this all-Protestant population was a single Roman Catholic family who had to worship outside the community. Any Protestant-Catholic division was minimized by the good-spirited acceptance of the Protestant majority by the Catholic family, and the respect given to the Catholics for their religious preference. They were part of the community. Thus, though differences could be listed, the community was really one of a closely-defined, single religious mind. God was in Heaven and all was right with the world. Pay homage, do unto others, and live quietly. This was not diversity. This was really a very single-minded philosophy.

Education in the community was even more homogeneous. Most of the people were the products of the local high school. The school was small—only three rooms in the entire building until some additions were made in the late 1940s. But the educational requirements were demanding, with agriculture and home economics programs complementing the more traditional academic courses. While only a small number of graduates continued into higher education, students were well prepared for life in the community. Individual success is testimony to the high school preparation. The needs of the community were served by the training, and the cycle of life continued, repeating for a new generation the tried and true ways of the past.

Upon reflection, Blooming Glen, circa 1945, had an ample supply of good-spirited, God-fearing people. Yet, it was also a town without a great deal of worldly sophistication. In addition to its homogeneous make-up, Blooming Glen was quite isolated. There was no cultural center of any kind, no movie theater or high school auditorium. A community highlight, the high school dramatic presentations, were performed in the rented auditorium at nearby Souderton High School, since the only public building, a small community hall, had been turned over to the high school and remodeled to house the popular agricultural courses offered by the school system.

Also, there were no train or trolley connections to neighboring communities. This was truly an isolated,

rural island. Such an environment, tied to the past with
traditional values and small-town virtues, seemed a likely
place for parochial visions, a likely place for a skeptical, if
not hostile, reaction to anything that was radically different. A revolutionary social experiment was about to begin
in this community. Would basic goodness and common
decency triumph, or would residents reflect the ongoing
prejudices of the time? Could this community meet the
challenge of a new day?

In the spring of 1945, a telephone call initiated a
chain of events that drastically changed the life of the Yoders
and, eventually, the community itself. An excited neighbor,
Katie Moyer, came to our door that spring evening, report-
ing that Pearl Buck was calling. Like many of the families
in Blooming Glen, we did not have our own phone at that
time, so it was not unusual for us to receive a call at our
neighbor's phone. However, it was most unusual for Pearl
Buck to call. I was not aware of Pearl Buck's importance at
that time, though I knew her name because she had moved
into a quaint farmhouse a few miles from Blooming Glen
in 1934.

Over the years, the homestead had undergone many
stages of remodeling. One of the new additions was a long,
winding farm lane. My father had worked on that project
during his summer job at the stone quarry in 1941. He
reported on this grand estate, and whetted my family's
curiosity. Like many of the families in the area, we drove
by to see the local marvel. Though quite young at the time,
I recall the impression left by the swimming pool, the
tennis court, and the massive house, and knew that a
special person was in our community. As my dad hurried
off to the neighbor's house that evening, I remember him
muttering about the bad joke someone was playing at our
neighbor's expense, and that we "better get a phone of our
own."

But it wasn't a joke. Pearl Buck was on the line and
she wanted to meet with my father concerning a part-time
teaching position. They met the next day. Pearl Buck wished

to employ a summer tutor for her four children of primary school age. The school superintendent, John Grasse, had recommended my dad and had given her our neighbor's telephone number. My father, who had always done summer work in the local stone quarry, decided this was a rare opportunity and more in keeping with his training, so he accepted the position. For the next four summers, he spent part of every day with the four Walsh children. (Pearl Buck was a pen name. She was legally Mrs. Richard Walsh, the wife of the editor of the John Day Publishing House.)

During these summers, my father would regularly take me to the Walsh estate. I was the same age as the Walsh children and would share in the varied activities. Mrs. Walsh was interesting in a wide range of experiences for the children, and so she insisted that sports and chores be part of the daily schedule. We planted flowers; we washed the family cars; we picked weeds; we scrubbed the swimming pool. We played baseball; we swam (I first learned to swim in the Walsh pool); we hit tennis balls; we rode horses (not I). It was an active time and a most memorable time. Sometimes we would sit under an old shade tree and listen to stories, told with excitement and emotion by my dad. His tales ranged from the classics, like *Treasure Island*, to an occasional shocker like *Room for One More*, to history and sports anecdotes.

Through my dad's memory, Red Grange, Connie Mack's Philadelphia Athletics, Kit Carson, Charles Lindbergh, and many more became heroes for all of us. In addition, there were frequent trips to the museums and historic sites, the Children's Theatre in Philadelphia, or baseball games at old Shibe Park. I was always included in these outings and came to know all of the Walshes quite well. Also, my mother and sister were invited to other functions at the Walsh homestead. Picnics, Christmas parties, tennis matches, or special July Fourth fireworks brought the Yoder and Walsh families into close contact. It was an unusual contact because, though social distance was always present, a clear, mutual respect emerged. In fact, we became friends, and this friendship became the basis for changes that were about to take place in the Yoder family.

— Chapter 3 —

THE BEGINNING

"We consider David to be the finest child we've had in the agency." What an endorsement, but it made no difference. The New York adoption agency with the gifted child failed to find a home for him. A letter to Pearl Buck in late fall 1948 explained the dilemma. The situation was heart-wrenching. David, a tiny East Indian-American had reached an age that made him ineligible to continue in the agency's adoption program. He had to be placed somewhere immediately. His predicament was a sad irony: East Indian families rejected him because he was half-American; American families rejected him because he was half-Indian. Here was a healthy, handsome, obviously bright one-year-old—the kind of child countless American couples were seeking, except his skin was the wrong color, his heritage blurred. Since he had no parents, but he had very dark skin, the agency had discovered a single option—place him in a black orphanage. The agency letter to Pearl Buck explained the circumstances. If she could not help, David would go to that orphanage.

Pearl Buck's reaction could be predicted by anyone who knew her. First she was angry. "A child with no place to lay its head? . . . a child no one wanted? . . . How could this be?" Then, she got on the telephone and spoke to many friends. It was true. No one wanted a mixed-blood child. Adoption policies required child and parent sameness, even matching hair and eye color; ethnic and racial matches were even more important. Apparently prospective parents agreed with this policy. David had no parental match. So Pearl Buck took the final step. She accepted responsibility for the child—not to adopt, but to place. On numerous occasions, I heard her explain, "I had no personal prejudices toward black Americans, but felt it would be very wrong to raise an East Indian child as a black child in a land that was so viciously anti-black. I knew I could find a way to care for him." The agency was not as optimistic, and they told her so. Still she said, "Send me the child."

Pearl Buck now asked her family to consider the problem, but they could find no easy solution. To begin with, both of the Walshes felt they were too old to become parents of a small child. Likewise, they didn't know how many children would need homes, though already a second child, about to be born and definitely unwanted, was brought to their attention. With the Christmas season approaching, the anticipated joys of the holidays were a stark contrast to the sad plight of the forsaken children. There could be no happy celebrations if the children's needs went unfulfilled. So all of the Walshes agreed the children must come to them until a permanent home could be found.

Perhaps influenced by the spirit of the season, Pearl Buck got an idea. If no existing family wanted these babies, why not create a family? The more they talked, the better they liked the idea. This would be a typical family, not an orphanage or even a foster home. The children would have the name of the parents; the Walshes could, in turn, fill the role of grandparents. The Walsh children would be young aunts and uncles, or perhaps cousins, depending upon the age of the children to be adopted, since older Asiatic-American children might also join the family. It was an exciting and defining moment.

Now they needed support and personal counsel. Pearl Buck turned to Margaret Fischer, a close friend, who had demonstrated in previous times that she shared similar love and concern for children. She hoped the Fischers would be the first recruits for her noble cause. As Mrs. Fischer remembers it, she and her husband were invited to the Walsh estate, expecting a typical social evening of dinner and conversation. Over dinner they discovered there was a specific purpose for the evening. Mrs. Walsh explained that she needed their help. She told them of the two babies and their sad predicament. She expressed her belief that many needed help. She had decided to create a family for these unloved ones and had a couple in mind who could become the parents. Her first home would be followed by as many as would be needed to take care of all the children. She was ambitious, enthusiastic, and confident. She knew this could be done, and it had to be done. Could they help her? After dinner neither of the women were particularly pleased with each husband's lack of enthusiasm for the proposed project. Apparently, Richard Walsh agreed with the first step—helping the initial babies—but felt the total project was too ambitious. However, within a week, each had convinced her respective mate to join in. In this way, the first supporters were recruited.

Kermit Fischer, local businessman and respected community leader, was not only converted to the project, but eventually became an extremely active participant. He frequently came to Welcome House on Saturday mornings to visit with the family. He shared his ideas on life, encouraged us all to pursue our goals, and was a constant source of guidance and influence for the maturing family. In addition, most of the Welcome House children became summer employees of his Fischer and Porter plant in Hatboro, thus adding to the financial and emotional security of the family members. The employment not only provided financial reward and the work experience for my brothers and sisters, but also served as a visible entry of formerly unrepresented, ethnically different workers into the community at large. It followed the frequent pattern of an uncle helping his relatives, but in this case the significance was far greater than mere financial help. This was local, ethnic assimilation and it made a difference. Kermit Fischer understood this. He was a true friend and a major reason for the success of Welcome House.

With the Fischers as partners, Pearl Buck confidently took the next step. She turned to the couple she had in mind—my parents. Another telephone call went out to the Yoders. This time it rang in our house. Since we now had our own telephone, and as is the wont in many households, the youngest member frequently rushes to answer the ring. As I answered, I was quite surprised to hear Pearl Buck on the line. My dad took the receiver and discovered she again had a prospective assignment for him. It seemed urgent. A few days later, my parents went to the Walsh home for a conference. It was an early evening in December 1948. When my parents returned a few hours later, they were clearly excited and said they had some things to share with us; then they would ask us a potentially life-changing question.

I'll never forget that moment. My dad said that Mrs. Walsh had spoken of many things, but central to her comments was a sad tale of two unwanted Asiatic-American children, and probably many others as yet unknown to her. She said that something had to be done for these unfortunates. My dad went on to say that Mrs. Walsh also felt we were the finest family she had ever encountered; that my sister was an amazing and talented young woman, and I was the best little boy she knew. (Some slight exaggeration on her part here, I suppose.) She was convinced that our family, well-adjusted and secure, could assume responsibility for the tiny, unwanted children. She wanted us to agree to be the family that would take these lovable but unloved ones into its heart and home; not just take them in, but help to plan for their needs and their future. I confess now that it was not a difficult decision. My parents were already convinced that it was something we should do. My sister and I joined in our parents' enthusiasm for the idea.

Encouragement from a few close friends and approval by our family doctor concluded our consideration. Within a week, my parents gave a positive reply. Mrs. Walsh was quite happy about this and said we would be informed of all developments, and my parents were to be included in any major decisions that had to be made.

All was proceeding quite nicely. Pearl Buck now had the parents, but she needed additional persons to join a Welcome House Board of Trustees—people who could help financially, people who could bring prestige, people who could bring ideas. She thought of Oscar Hammerstein, also a resident of Bucks County. Again, dinner at the Walshes Green Hill Farms was the means of contact. Oscar and Dorothy Hammerstein were the invited guests.

Dorothy Hammerstein later commented: "Out of the blue, Pearl Buck invited us for dinner. She brought out this handsome little half-Indian boy she wanted to get adopted." Apparently, Oscar first thought that Pearl Buck wanted them to adopt David, but by this time, the Yoders had already consented to be the parents. Pearl Buck needed the Hammersteins to help—not to adopt. Since Oscar had recently revealed his interest in bi-racial relationships in the Broadway musicals, *South Pacific* and *The Flower Drum Song*, the Hammersteins were most likely prospects. They eagerly joined in the project and became very involved with a variety of fund raisers—fashion shows, raffles, and a Jane Pickens concert.

Oscar was a generous supporter throughout his life and was elected president of the Welcome House Board in 1950. He occasionally stopped by Welcome House to see the family. His time and financial support were invaluable. His name helped considerably in gaining further support and public approval of the venture. Mrs. Hammerstein was to become Aunt Dorothy to the children, and she frequently visited Welcome House and became a good friend to Mother. Recruiting the Hammersteins was one more important step in the growth of Welcome House.

The Board expansion continued. David and Lois Burpee were friends of the Hammersteins. They happily joined and brought the wealth and influence of a major corporation, the Burpee Seed Company. Bucks County Judge Edward and Muriel Biester brought local prestige and political power to the Board. Dr. Frederick Stamm was a minister with a book published by John Day Publishers.

He and his wife were delighted and honored to be appointed to the Board. And finally, the James Micheners completed the original circle. The exact order for bringing all these couples onto the Board is not clear, and not really significant.

Pearl Buck had solicited Michener's opinion on her Welcome House idea soon after she heard of David's predicament, probably about the time she spoke to the Hammersteins. Michener's endorsement led to the invitation to join the Board. They were very important additions. Like Hammerstein, his feelings on race relations were public record. He lived in nearby Bedminster in those years, so he was a local celebrity who added stature, and courted local acceptance of the project. All of the Board members brought specific talents and enthusiastic commitment to the social experiment. Each offered their financial support (specific amounts not available, but it must have been considerable), and each shared of themselves through visits and social engagements, such as picnics for the family or parties for the children.

The women of the Board also gave formal and informal support. The Welcome House Thrift Shop in Doylestown, fashion shows and concerts, and public raffles succeeded primarily because of the Board women and the volunteers they recruited. Also, Lois Burpee, Muriel Biester, and Dorothy Hammerstein, because they lived nearby, would often come to Welcome House and lend a helping hand in the daily activities. It was a prestigious group, but they lent much more than their names. They gave their time, money, and love. Welcome House would not have made it without them.

In its initial meeting, the newly constituted Board accepted the principal guidelines defined by Pearl Buck and Margaret Fischer. For example, they agreed Welcome House was to be a family, not a foster home or orphanage. There should be adequate financial support to make this a comfortable home. There had to be emotional as well as financial support for this undertaking because it was feared that this was a social situation that could produce negative local reaction. And, it was vigorously asserted that a vital social need was being addressed, with ramifications that would undoubtedly go far beyond the two original children.

The Board realized that since Asian-American orphans were not at that time placed through the existing adoption process, the Welcome House solution (creating families and providing financial support for them) might be necessary for a long time, considering the difficulty encountered in finding a home for David. But such a sobering conclusion didn't diminish Pearl Buck's confidence. I heard her say on many occasions, "We will create 100 Welcome Houses if we must. These rejected ones will have a home." It's difficult to imagine how finances for "100 Welcome Houses" would have been forthcoming, but such uncertainty did not prevent the Board from moving forward. They had two particular problems, both pressing yet difficult to solve. First, they had to meet the needs of the Yoders and the new family; second, they had to consider what to do once the Yoder family was complete. Could they hope to come to the aid of the multitude of children who were out there, similar to David? Such concerns weighed heavily on the Board as they launched a forthright attack on a sad social injustice with vision and open-minded plans. It was a time of cautious optimism.

The Yoders, too, were in a time of uncertainty. We had agreed to a new life with virtually no specific details decided. How large would our family become? Where would we reside? What kind of financial support would be offered? None of this was known, but we plunged ahead with great enthusiasm and anticipation. The next months were quite a new experience for us; yet, as time went by, I never recall a moment of doubt. From the beginning, there was complete commitment to this cause. We knew we were taking a momentous step, but we always felt it was a rare opportunity to do something special—to provide a normal home to small, unfortunate children in great need.

Pearl Buck and the Board pressed on. Having found parents and a group of influential supporters, Pearl Buck's next step was a very logical one. Local leaders from the two nearby villages, Blooming Glen and Dublin, were asked to come to her home to discuss a particular issue that required their involvement. Occasional meetings of this sort were successfully used to attract Welcome House supporters. *My Several Worlds* records the first gathering in the Walsh living room. Most of the Dublin and Blooming Glen business and church leaders attended and heard Pearl Buck outline the proposed plans for an international family in their community. Then she asked these people if they could support her in this endeavor. Local Dublin grocer Herbert Stauffer, a long-time friend of the Yoders and a fellow church member, responded with the apparent spirit of the group. In his Pennsylvania Dutch manner he stated, "We won'dt only be willin,' we will be proudt to have the childtern."

I recall a similar get-together after Welcome House began. This time, in the Welcome House living room, and with most of the same people, the support from the leaders was reaffirmed. "We will be proud to have the children" was again the echoed sentiment of the meeting. With such community spirit, Welcome House seemed bound to succeed.

In retrospect, there can be little doubt that Pearl Buck knew the community leaders would support her, but it was her genius which realized that forming this group at the outset of Welcome House guaranteed a local elite that would aid in overcoming any local problems, should they arise. It is impossible to know if these people ever had to use their influence to silence any critics, but it is true they were there if needed. And certainly, their participation may have thwarted any resistance to Welcome House before it ever began.

The international family was close to reality. Parents had been found; a board of directors had been formed; local community leaders enthusiastically endorsed the idea; people of means gave indication that financial support would be forthcoming. Could Welcome House encounter so little difficulty?

The pieces were falling into place, but now an immediate concern was a house for the family. Our home in Blooming Glen was quite small. One child would find no space, and who knew how many more would follow? Three small second-floor bedrooms, a small kitchen, dining room, and tiny living room on a lot that was less than thirty feet wide was clearly an inadequate site for the new family.

At this moment, one more of many unplanned but fortuitous events took place. A small fifteen-acre farm was unexpectedly put up for sale. Called the Bittersweet Farm, it was the lone island of real estate that remained within the acreage of Pearl Buck's holdings. These fifteen acres were immediately adjacent to the Pearl Buck Estate itself, and seemed the ideal location for the new family. A contract for $25,000 was struck. My parents were informed and were in total agreement with this purchase.

I remember our first trip to the Bittersweet Farm (soon to be renamed Welcome House). Our parents, my sister, her fiancé Charles Strouse, and I were invited to visit while the owners still lived there. It was an eye-opening experience for me. Suddenly, we were in the midst of this mammoth dwelling with a living room that was larger than the first floor of our Blooming Glen house. It was overwhelming, to say the least. The stone farmhouse, built in the early 1800s, and currently valued at more than $300,000, included the large eighteen-foot-by-thirty-foot living room with a stone fireplace, a large dining room, a large but not modernized kitchen, and a den with a walk-in fireplace. On the second floor were five large bedrooms and two baths. The third floor had four bedrooms and one bath. Although the house was beginning to show its age, it was a veritable castle by our standards. We could replace the peeling paint and faded wallpaper, using our own labor. My dad and all of us older brothers painted the house from top to bottom, inside and outside, in the succeeding summers. Old bathrooms and a 1920s kitchen did not diminish our enthusiasm. Later, some inexpensive remodeling corrected that problem. In every way, the house fit the Welcome House needs to perfection. All of us felt a great wave of excitement; we had taken another gigantic step.

As I think back upon this first encounter with our residence-to-be, I realize that in my young mind, the imposing physical presence of this large, magnificent house was paramount. But as the years passed and I reflect upon life in Welcome House, I see the house, not in this physical sense, but as a home, a place where so many good things happened. True, it was a wonderful house—large, sturdy, warm, but it was an even more wonderful home—loving, nurturing, teaching. This is the reality I hope to capture.

Next, we furnished the house. This was a mini-lesson, I believe, in how my parents felt about their commitment to Welcome House. It is clear that much about our lifestyle was improved by the move to Welcome House. It is equally clear that Welcome House was not a money-making venture for our parents. For example, all of our Blooming Glen furniture was moved to Welcome House. But, due to the difference in the size of the houses, only a small portion of the house would be furnished by the move. However, on the night of our visit to the Bittersweet Farm, I can hear one of the owners asking my parents if they needed any of the furniture that filled many of the rooms. Three bedroom suites, a den couch, a stuffed chair, and a number of wooden chairs (including two very stately captain's chairs) were among the items that they wished to sell. I know my parents felt the cost would be too high, but when the owner said, "twenty-five dollars," the sale was quickly consummated.

Let me share a brief word about that experience. The Bittersweet Farm was quite a contrast to the new home it was about to become. The owners were two elderly brothers and a sister, probably all in their seventies, maybe older (at age twelve, everyone over thirty seems old). But they were kindly souls who exhibited their good spirits in a number of ways. One of the brothers showed me these great balls of silver which he had made from the silver wrappings of chewing gum. For those too young to remember, chewing gum sticks, in an earlier age, were individually wrapped in paper lined with silver to preserve freshness. Over many years, the old gentleman had carefully separated the silver from the paper and gathered them into balls larger than a softball and probably as heavy as a bowling ball. He had five of these silver balls, and when I showed a fascination with his collection, he gave me one, saying something like, "This will remind you of us when you move in with your new family. I know you will enjoy this home just like we did." I sincerely believe that the furniture was provided with the same spirit. In my opinion, the owners recognized the purpose of Welcome House and wanted to provide both a memory from their past, and a contribution to our future. This is just one more example of the consistent support that Welcome House received.

Through the years, my parents regularly added to the Welcome House furnishings, and I'd estimate that about ninety per cent of the furniture was provided by my parents. Some was donated, and a few items were purchased through the Board when a particular need arose. And, as in everything that was to become part of the Welcome House experience; there was no separation into the Yoder belongings versus the Welcome House belongings. This was a common endeavor and one that had little concern for mundane details.

One of the donated pieces was the dining room table that opened to more than twenty feet and included a dozen chairs and a giant server. The table was a major addition to Welcome House as the family grew larger and larger, and was also frequently opened to its full extent for the many dinners my parents had for relatives and guests. The dining room table was a central part of our family life, as it is in many households, but it also serves as evidence of the commitment underway as Welcome House came into existence. A telephone call came to Pearl Buck offering a massive, but functional, table that could serve a large family if the dining room were big enough. She and my mother made the journey to a home near Doylestown to investigate. My mother later reported the predicament of this investigation. The only access to the house was on a rope bridge that crossed a rather actively running stream. Mrs. Walsh took one look at the bridge and refused to use it. My mother carefully crossed on the bridge, then watched as Mrs. Walsh solved her problem. She hiked up her skirt and waded through waist-deep water to reach the other side. The table proved to be worth the effort. I never thought to ask, so I don't know how that heavy piece of furniture made its way over that stream, but I do know that it got to Welcome House, served our family for over twenty years, and was always a reminder of the multitude of ways people contributed to the needs of Welcome House, and the exertions required for its success.

Financial agreements were reached, based on trust and need, not by any formal contract. Basically, Welcome House trustees provided the house, a car, food expenses, and a small allowance for my mother. She also had a helper to pitch in with whatever needed to be done. Much of the cooking and cleaning was covered by the assistant. In turn, my parents contributed all their resources and my dad's income to the common goal—a happy, normal home, big and comfortable, but hardly luxurious. Certainly there were increased material blessings for the original Yoders, but there was also a new set of personal demands and a massive time commitment. My mother, in particular, was tied to the changing life style. Within two years, she had five children under the age of three who required much attention, leaving her little freedom to carry on any active social life. She didn't complain, because her life had greater meaning, although she certainly had less time for herself.

The benefits of Welcome House were shared. My parents had improved certain aspects of their lives, but certainly they had not discovered a magic formula for accumulating personal riches. No clearer proof of this truth can be made than to recognize that, at the time of his death in 1968, my father's net worth was the death benefit from his teaching pension (approximately $50,000), a two-year-old car, and the Welcome House furniture (approximately $5,000). My mother, who died in 1982, fared even less well. She had used up Dad's $50,000 stipend, having shared much of it with the children. A Welcome House pension and social security provided her with about $10,000 annually, and she spent her last years living with her adopted daughter, interspersed with month-long visits to the rest of her children to reduce her living costs. At her death, her life insurance covered her funeral expenses, and all of her children pitched in to pay off her bills.

These personal facts are included here only to illustrate that for some, success is not measured by the accumulation of material blessings. My parents' lives were dedicated to sharing, not accumulating. By their humane instincts and their religious guidelines, they followed a path that brought life and happiness to many. Without sanctimonious public display and without truly calculating the personal rewards, they believed in the words of the Gospel of Matthew: "Do not lay up for yourselves treasures on earth, where moth and rust consume and where thieves break through, but lay up for yourselves treasures in heaven where neither moth nor rust consumes and where thieves do not break through and steal. For where your treasure is, there will your heart be also." Any who knew my parents can tell you where their hearts were.

During the last weeks of 1948 and the early weeks of 1949, much was happening. These were the times when each moment added something different to the Welcome House configuration. For example, a formal application for a charter had to be completed and accepted by the state. The original charter called for the children of Welcome House to be American born and of mixed Far Eastern and American parentage. In 1953, as the Welcome House office was able to place children in adoptive homes, this American-born clause was stricken and the agency would eventually become a conduit for any children, but, true to its origin, particularly hard-to-place children.

And so the time was here. All the important preparations had taken place. The efforts of Pearl Buck, my parents, and a host of supporters were about to reach fruition. Something very unique in American life was about to begin.

— Chapter 4 —

THE FAMILY FORMS

David arrived first. It was in December 1948. The unwanted one came to the door of the Walsh estate because all was not yet in readiness at the new Yoder home. Pearl Buck described his arrival, accompanied by the social worker.

> *One night, deep in darkness, the doorbell rang and there stood the good woman with a little boy in a red snowsuit in her arms. He was sucking his thumb and his eyes were huge and tragic, with the look that always reveals a child without home and parents. I took him in my arms, and he was as motionless in the arms of a stranger as a bird is in the hand of a human being. "I'm sorry I can't stay," the good woman said, "but you'll understand."*
>
> *She went away and the child's eyes did not change. He knew it did not matter who came or went. He belonged to nobody. At that moment, anger faded from my heart and love began. I took him upstairs to my own room, I undressed him and bathed him warm and clean, and put on a pair of wooly pajamas that I had found in an attic chest. He uttered not a sound, he did not make a move to protest. He did not cry. It was I who cried because he was so desperately brave. I rocked him a while and he looked at me with those great dark eyes, wondering who I was and why he was here. I put him in the crib beside my bed, and he lay, not sleeping, but sucking his thumb again. When I was ready for bed, I turned on the night light so that he could see me and know that I was ready for his small brown hand, extended tentatively through the bars of the crib. Again and again that little hand came toward me in the night, and each time I received it into my own.*

And so it began for the unwanted and unloved children. David, the impossible-to-place child, was here. There were many more to come. Each would bring a similar sad story, but each would find the same warmth and love.

Within a few days, it would be our turn. I remember the evening in December that all of us went to meet David for the first time. In essence this was the origin of Welcome House; this was the beginning of our new family.

David sat in the living room of the Walsh home by the side of his grandmother, or "Gran," as all the Welcome House children would know her. It was immediately apparent that here was an unusual child. He combined the expected and natural evidence of a frightened fifteen-month-old child with a bright-eyed curiosity that spelled intelligence and friendliness. In the following weeks, before Welcome House was ready, we regularly took David on outings: to church, to visit relatives, to dinner. On most of these trips David and I would be in the back seat, and we became immediate friends. His particular affinity for me continued on into the days when we moved to Welcome House. After he learned to climb from his crib, he generally managed to find his way to my room and treat me to an early morning wake-up call, wearing a wet diaper that he settled on body, face, or wherever he could climb. Now David was here and the Welcome House family had begun; there was no turning back.

Leon was born the day after Christmas, 1948. He, too, had to spend his first weeks at the Walsh house. Our first meeting was also in the Walsh living room. Leon lay in a screened port-a-crib that could be rolled outside, although why it was used in January, with Pennsylvania weather, I never knew. Peeking through the screen, we saw a cherubic baby whose disposition was always to be happy and smiling (well, almost always). As an infant, he didn't usually join us on our family excursions in those pre-Welcome House weeks, but we saw him frequently. Mother went to see both Leon and David during this time and her love and care were essential for the new children in their new environment. Our family of four was now an international family of six, and nationality make-up was now three, since Leon had Chinese background. But we were still a family without a home.

Finally, in March of 1949, the move took place. With our new family we fell into a whole new routine of life. My father and I made our morning exit to school, where he continued his teaching and coaching. I was finishing the last months of eighth grade, eagerly anticipating the summer on our new farm and a Fall entry into the big time, Hilltown High School. My sister Charlotte, having graduated from high school the previous year, and after an emotional period of decision, had rejected her music scholarship to our church college in Bluffton, Ohio. This, too, proved to be one of those fortuitous acts, because now in March she could resign from her job and stay home and become Mother's first helper through these unknown, early days of Welcome House.

For nearly a year, this was the routine. My mother fulfilled her role to perfection. The family was thriving and developing. Pearl Buck, as grandmother, stopped by regularly to feed or play with the little ones. Mr. Walsh, while less involved, was still a kindly and supportive grandfather. The Walsh family regularly had the two babies come visit for a day or an afternoon. From all the Walshes—Gran, Granddaddy, and the Walsh children—and from all the Yoders, large doses of love and attention were being dispersed. As a result, the Welcome House children were showing all indications of a happy, normal existence.

The next to enter the family was Sumi. A little, frightened Japanese child, she seemed to be in dire need of love and attention. Once more, late in 1949, our family gathered at the Walsh estate. This time we met in the dining room and Sumi was cowering in one of the large captain's chairs that surrounded the dining room table. Near tears, she seemed to yearn for invisibility as the Yoder family encircled her. I can still see my mother reach down and gently lift her. There was an almost mystical union as Sumi melted into the safety of Mother's arms. From that day on there was always a special relationship between Mother and daughter, and I can't imagine any biological dyad being any closer. Sumi came home with us and another link in the family chain was added.

Through the winter and spring of 1950, the new family continued to adjust and flourish. The babies were not difficult ones. Leon occasionally needed to have his crib gently shaken at night to quell a crying spell. Sumi developed a crying technique where she could hold her breath so long that it caused Mother to panic on occasion. In an unfair and somewhat facetious fashion, some of her brothers have claimed that this was the beginning of Sumi's special status in the family. In truth, as the only female among the smaller ones, she did have a one-to-one relationship with Mother and Dad, while the young boys were more regularly treated as a unit. As for David, he had very bowed legs and hurried about on pigeon toes in a style that eventually required special straps and corrective shoes. Mother burst into tears when she first saw the cumbersome contraption. His later success as a varsity athlete indicated that the correction, a year-long burden, worked. Thus unusual circumstances were addressed, a routine of everyday life was established, and, from all indications, a happy family was in place.

Gran Walsh's early influence could be felt by the family. Without creating tension, she nevertheless indicated that certain things had to be done for the children. Of crucial importance was the food. In an age that was less aware of the value of diet and nutrition, Mrs. Walsh placed much emphasis on eating properly. Fresh orange juice was a must, and I remember some of the early morning hours, squeezing and straining juice for the first day's bottles. As the children grew, she also emphasized the value of lean meats, fresh vegetables, and whole grain bread. I thought of her beliefs some years ago when reading *Letter From*

Peking, a book she admitted was based on personal experience. In the book there is a passage in which the heroine compares her noonday lunch to that of her hired helper.

> *He is a silent fellow, a Vermonter, lank and lean, his teeth gone too early from a wretched diet which nevertheless he would not improve. He looks upon my brown bread and green salads with distaste and refusal and though I press him to share my luncheon, he sits apart and munches what he calls lunch meat between two slabs of cheap bread, which I consider not bread but a solidified form of white flour and water.*

In fiction or reality, she spoke with conviction. From her, we all learned and benefited.

The first year passed without incident. I am sure there must have been times when my parents felt that the new responsibilities were heavy, and that life would have been simpler had we remained in our little Blooming Glen house. Undoubtedly, our new life was drastically different. It was more demanding in many ways. In our Blooming Glen days, our family routine was fast-paced, but well scheduled and regular. Dad's teaching and coaching responsibilities were long and hard, but they had a beginning and an end. These same demands continued when Welcome House began, but the added duties as father to a growing household created a backbreaking schedule, and he did it all incredibly well. (Although as indicative of a different generation, I never saw him change a diaper or give a bottle to the babies.)

Mother's life was even more altered. Her job in nearby Souderton was very specific. She was a store clerk with authority to buy specific merchandise for different departments (women's apparel, pocketbooks, etc.). She enjoyed her work, was reasonably paid, and gained much personal satisfaction from her efforts. Her day ended when the store closed since my sister and I were responsible for most of the household chores. My dad would occasionally prepare some evening meals. Dried beef gravy on sweet potatoes was his specialty. (I hated it then, love it now.

Nostalgia, I guess.) Two or three times a week we would eat at Goldie's Diner in nearby Dublin, an inexpensive but wonderful restaurant that I loved (many food choices, no dishes to wash). Now Mother's day didn't end at five o'clock. In fact, it really didn't end because she was on twenty-four-hour call. The added work, the added hours, the added pressures left no observable marks on my parents. I sensed no depression or yearning for the old days. Welcome House was a specific place that seemed to bring good spirit to all who partook of it; family and friends all substantiate this contention. Simply described, it was a time of great joy. Then an announcement in late winter caused some pause for reflection.

Mrs. Walsh came to tell my parents that the Board had been approached by an orphanage in Detroit. Three children—two brothers and a sister—had been orphaned by a terminal illness and a traffic accident in rapid succession and needed a home. The children, whose father was Chinese, were fifteen, thirteen, and eleven years of age. It was the age of the new children that prompted an initial concern. How strongly forged were the values and ways of children this age? Would they be difficult to manage, and thus have a negative effect on the happily adjusting three small babies in the family?

Life was currently running smoothly and without trauma. But, my parents would never have allowed such concerns to do harm to children in need, and so they accepted the challenge without objection, indeed, with enthusiasm. Now fourteen, I was less convinced. Reflecting upon my reaction, I can see that the presence of a fifteen-year-old male had awakened some feelings of territorial protection and/or sibling rivalry. At that time, though, I couldn't really explain it. I just knew I felt differently about the entry of a fifteen-year-old into our lives than I had about the little ones. This was the only moment I had questions about our new life.

On a clear Sunday in June 1950, Frank, Ray, and Lillian arrived. I remember sitting on the front porch waiting for their car. Finally it came, and three children and the social worker got out. Each wore a colorful, Hawaiian-type shirt with slacks. Strangely, my first reaction to each was that they seemed older than their announced ages. But I had no negative reactions. We all moved into the living room for our first conversations. It was awkward at first. All were shy and a bit nervous. Handsome and polite, each made a very positive first impression. I was most interested in fifteen-year-old Frank, and remember him as being shorter than I, but definitely more muscular. In those first minutes, I could find nothing to substantiate any of my earlier concerns; in fact, if anything, I was feeling quite positive.

After the initial meeting and polite conversation, Dad suggested that I take Frank outside and show him the property. This seemed like a good idea, and Frank immediately wanted to go look at the barn. I found out later that he had hoped to start some sort of boy's club in conjunction with some friends he left behind in Detroit and was curious to see if the barn would be suitable for a club house. We climbed up into the hayloft, and Frank promptly jumped out the barn door to the ground, about fifteen feet below.

He turned and said, "Come on."

Shocked by his daring, my only reaction was a quiet, "Holy smoke," and a quick exit down the steps to join him for the rest of the tour.

The first summer tended to prove that all my fears were premature and without merit. Each new sibling moved easily into the family circle. Lillian proved to be a big help with all the household chores; Ray was a good helper in the garden; Frank and I had the good fortune to be hired by Mrs. Walsh to work in her garden or do projects around Welcome House that were approved by Dad. The Walshes had established this working plan for their children as the replacement for the organized summer activities that my dad had formerly provided. So Frank and I worked twenty to thirty hours per week at the rate of thirty-five cents an hour, and we thought we were on Easy Street. I never saw so much money at one time, and Frank began to develop his entrepreneurial habits, saving and also finding other ways of adding to his wealth (raising and selling gladiolas, catching pigeons for the local gun clubs, catching live rabbits for the game commission, etc.). His current success as a businessman was probably forged in these early enterprises.

One of our projects, a carefully constructed bridge over a dry ditch that occasionally filled with running rain water, was a major effort. The bridge completed the path between the Walsh estate and Welcome House and was a lifeline to the Walsh's swimming pool and television set that were always available for the Yoders' use. Constructed of cement blocks and heavy planks, the bridge was the crowning achievement of our summer work. We were especially proud when Gran Walsh made the mile hike across the path to inspect our handiwork. She judged that it was a most meritorious accomplishment and would stand the test of time. Her words were prophetic, for at a recent family reunion more than thirty-five years later, Frank and I struggled through thick underbrush (the path long gone) to find the remains of our bridge. The cement blocks remain, though the wood has now rotted away. Though hardly of earth-shaking consequence, it was a most poignant reminder of the good times we shared.

For me, the most memorable event of that first summer happened about a month after Frank arrived. Dad suggested that I organize a swimming party at Menlo Park in neighboring Perkasie. He thought Frank should meet some of the young friends who would be his schoolmates in the next year. This seemed like a good idea, and so one hot summer afternoon we journeyed to this neighboring town about six miles from Welcome House. Ten or twelve of my friends were invited, and I remember walking out along the pool to greet those who had arrived before us, when suddenly I found myself flying through the air into the water. This unplanned dunking was a kind of embarrassing convention that placed you well down on the macho scale, I suppose. But before I could protest or make some excuse for my ineptitude, I found my attacker flying in beside me, muttering and stammering about an unfair dunking. I looked up to see Frank smiling on the pool's edge. Even though he was a newcomer and knew no one, Frank had responded on my behalf. It was at that moment, inane as it might sound now, that I realized I had a brother—a friend, a protector, a confidant.

For the next four years, until Frank graduated from high school and joined the Coast Guard, we couldn't have been closer. We shared our troubles; we shared our joys. We played on championship teams; we played on losing teams. We spent our summers (after the first one) working long and hard at Fischer and Porter in Hatboro, the company of Kermit Fischer, Welcome House supporter and surrogate uncle of the children. All in all, it was a truly joyous time for me, and I feel guilty now about my original unfounded apprehension. But it is clear to me now that I could always count on my brother. And though time and geography and family demands have kept us separated in these later years, I know that if I needed him for anything, my brother would be there. And he knows that it is likewise for him. No one can dunk us in the pool and get away with it.

Another child came to our door in December 1950. Bobby, age five, fresh from a military-styled orphanage, came marching into Welcome House in his military garb. For weeks, he constantly needed a familiar connection with the past, and wanted to wear his uniform. He remembers some of his pre-Welcome House years. Mostly, he remembers switching from foster home to foster home, finally ending up in the military school because, as Bobby claims, he was "too bad to stay in any private home." He remembers a rule in the military home that said no visitors on Sunday afternoon for those who are being disciplined. In his memory, he went a whole year without a visitor. It was from this environment that Bobby was rescued. After a short time, his early toughness was softened and he became one of the clan, happy and involved. Bobby's quick and easy smile and rumbling laugh that still is a part of him today made him an easy entry into the expanding family.

The following spring, ten-month-old Jackie arrived. Initially frightened, with long hair flowing down his neck and over his ears and forehead, he gave a quick first impression of a little old man. He was shy and quiet, and had a serious demeanor, but love and attention soon brought him into the family.

The last of the little ones arrived in the summer of 1952. The same age as Jackie, Paul was, however, quite a contrast. Wide-eyed and with a quick smile, he had a mischievous streak that has never left him. Jack and Paul, as the "babies" in the family, were the recipients of much attention. Without a doubt they were much loved and added one more page to the Welcome House story.

Only Scott, who would join us in 1958, was missing from the family portrait. And so by 1952 that portrait would include the following. Charlotte married and, about to begin her own family, lived a mile away and still helped Mother on occasion with specific chores: summer canning, special cleaning sessions, etc. Five of us were in public school. I was a junior in high school; Frank was a sophomore, Lillian in ninth grade, Ray in sixth grade, and Bobby was in third grade. The "little ones," as we older kids referred to them, broke down as follows: David, age five; Leon, age four; Sumi, age three and a half; Paul and Jack, two and a half. The racial make-up: one Korean (Jack); one Japanese (Sumi); two Indians (Paul and David); and the rest Chinese. Scott, who came to our family in 1958, was also Chinese-American. With him our family would be complete.

It seems to me the supreme irony of Welcome House that these early years of putting this number of East and West individuals into one family should be the exact years when East and West were in the process of splitting apart. The Communist bloc countries that followed the lead of the Soviet Union, the "Chinese hoards" that made the

Korean War such a cold war "hot spot," the "Red Menace" that gave Joe McCarthy his focal point for his own national notoriety—these were the judgments of many about the Eastern world and its wickedness. To use the conventional wisdom of that time, these were the people that gave in to Godless communism and threatened to take away our freedom. But in Pearl Buck's Welcome House, a loving couple and nine small unwanted children were offering a different scenario on how to accomplish satisfactory East/West relations—namely, larger doses of love and attention and blindness to the color distinctions that have for so long divided us. This, then, was the family. It is time now to follow some of the events that happened in the ensuing years.

Chapter 5

LIFE AT WELCOME HOUSE: THE EARLY YEARS

On the national scene, the 1950s were curious years as the post-war dichotomy continued. On one side, optimists emphasized the "nifty-fifties," and traditional ways were in vogue. We "liked" Ike, we loved baseball; what was good for General Motors was good for the country; panty raids were good for campus life; communists were bad; women, for the most part, were helpmates; God was in His heaven and all was right with the world. But we also had McCarthyism; we had a "police action" in Korea, Jack Kerouac was "on the road" and he didn't like Ike; C. Wright Mills didn't like the "power elite," or by association, General Motors; James Dean was a "rebel without a cause"; Marlon Brando, Montgomery Clift, and even more visibly, Elvis the Pelvis, were a new breed of celebrity, not "men in gray flannel suits," but irreverent, sexual, and in all ways, non-traditional.

David Halberstam in *The Fifties* writes that the fifties were in black and white and the sixties followed in living color. The birth control pill was one example of his film/television metaphor in action. Discovered in the fifties, the pill led to social change in the sixties. By Halberstam's analysis, the fifties had tradition, but the decade also had a substructure that paved the way for massive changes that followed.

Welcome House was a happy example of how past traditions and present changes can co-exist and somehow escape an emotional collision. Welcome House defied tradition with its enlightened racial make-up and its contribution to further changes in Asian-American life in this century. Yet Welcome House life revolved around very traditional values and goals for the family. Our parents constantly reminded us of the importance of family, church, school, and community. Rules of life ranged from "being good" at all times to being fair to everyone. Misbehavior was not tolerated, but having fun was encouraged. Having friends was more valuable than having money. Virtue was its own reward. A stitch in time saves nine. And on and on. Ben Franklin must have smiled as Welcome House developed because his maxims of life were certainly part of the Welcome House code of conduct. While emphasizing traditional morality, the demands were neither repressive nor illogical. Rather, they produced happiness and contentment.

By the early fifties, it was evident that the Yoders could fulfill their unusual assignment. Our parents showed how insignificant racial differences could be if one were tolerant, believed in equality, and practiced fairness. In such an environment the children flourished. By the time of Dwight Eisenhower's first election, the Welcome House family was all but complete (Scott arrived in 1958). To borrow from a past-President's coined word, "normalcy" described the family in action, at least as normal as a large international family could be.

Welcome House developed in a quiet way. Out in the country, two miles from Blooming Glen, one mile from Dublin, there was opportunity to fashion a life for the children without a great deal of interference. In this setting, traditional ways counted more than the usual make-up of the family, and the way we succeeded confirms this view. Details of our life can be drawn from two distinct patterns. First, there were the routines we followed regularly. All family members had specific roles and contributed significantly to the Welcome House ways. Second, revealing anecdotes were a good measure of Welcome House life as they offer meaningful, unusual moments in our life and the strengths and purposes of the persons involved. Through these patterns, we discovered a strong family unit, a unit that had the self-esteem and maturity to function in a world that might not have been ready for it, at least at the time the family began.

The routines of our life were productive and interesting. Everyone did their part. For example, Mother directed the basic, daily needs of the family. Dad fulfilled his teaching responsibilities at school and became the respected father figure at home, always supporting Mother. We older kids were students, enjoyed our school life, and found no one who rejected or belittled the family's ethnic differences. The little ones formed their own "at home" nursery school and were nurtured successfully through these early Welcome House years. Our life revolved around these daily activities which were regularly punctuated by family celebrations (holidays, birthdays, picnics, etc.), family vacations, garden chores, ball games, church functions, family leisure (television, an occasional dinner out), and the like. Repeating these activities year after year, we established a way of life that shaped the children as they grew and matured. It was in many ways a typical life, even though the family composition was anything but. The internal efficiency of the family made possible by everyone's cooperation, provided a solid base for Welcome House to succeed within the larger community.

Welcome House success began with the children. Whether they sensed at an early age that they were different from others outside the family and thus were drawn together, or whether there was just the good fortune of a coincidental lucky fit, the children did get along very well from the very beginning. Truthfully, there was little internal friction and much love and cooperation. Of course, the age differences of the children created some natural family groups: the young ones (five under five years of age), the middle twosome (ages seven and eleven), and the "wise" ones (ages fourteen, fifteen, and sixteen). Though these groupings produced a variety of different interests and activities within the family, we still functioned with ease and cooperation. This is particularly remarkable when you consider the trauma and emotion that occurs when one new infant is introduced into a family. Somehow, our parents were managing a whole nursery of cherubs, dealing with the demands of the pre-teenagers and controlling the impetuous immaturity of us, the high school students.

Cooperation was an obvious necessity to keep things running smoothly. We all had our duties and regularly pitched in to help with family needs at busy moments. Our sister Charlotte continued to be part of the Welcome House team. Though living in Blooming Glen and beginning a family of her own, she helped in many ways whenever called upon; for example, occasional cleaning, summer food preservation, taking the children to friends or parties, and so forth. Her successors as helpers for Mother, in sequence, Mary Histand, Marie Althouse, Nancy Histand, Jean Stutzman, and for a short time Fanny Kitchline, were loving persons, dedicated to Welcome House. Each one loved the children and treated them like family. They did whatever was asked of them—cleaning, cooking, babysitting—and it was done with enthusiasm as well as with love. I never heard my parents criticize the efforts of these dedicated young women. But at the heart and soul of the family were our parents. Their love, wisdom, and parenting ability overcame any obstacles that the unusual size or composition of this family might present.

This was Welcome House in the early fifties, a home with much love, much happiness, and much to look forward to. We went about our daily lives with high spirits and enthusiasm. It was a wonderful environment that had to be blessed. It was, to say the least, a joyous time.

Thinking about our everyday life, I must begin with our cornerstone, Mother. She was the constant presence, the person who had the greatest responsibilities, and the one who had to answer the beck and call of all the children, all the time. Mother was the one who also sacrificed the most for Welcome House because she had to give up so much of her personal life. Her successful and promising career in retail ended. How far she would have gone with this career is total speculation, but she was very good at her position and her employer was sad to have her leave. Now she was connected to the little children. Their time was her time and she served them with love and dedication. I know she did this happily and without resentment. But life away from home was limited for her. As an example, over the next four years my mother never was free to attend any of the dozens of athletic events (basketball, soccer, baseball) that my dad coached and we older brothers played in. It was only during my college days that she felt free to attend games, bringing along the younger children who had become six-, seven-, and eight-year-olds. As my brothers and sisters grew, we realized how much she had sacrificed during those early years, because she got much enjoyment from all of their high school and college performances (football injuries being the one exception).

There was an interesting, perhaps ironic, outcome from Mother's sacrifices for the Welcome House family. A few months before Pearl Buck contacted my parents with the Welcome House proposal, my mother suffered what was apparently a mild heart attack. She was not hospitalized, but was ordered to bedrest. Her condition was a concern when the Welcome House prospects were being considered.

My parents sought the advice of our family doctor, Francis Souder. He felt that Mother could manage this responsibility, but in keeping with the medical wisdom of the time, advised her not to run up and down steps and to use good judgment in not overexerting herself. Perhaps a nursery could be made on the first floor so afternoon naps could be downstairs and eliminate some of the running upstairs.

I remember that in those early years, I was frequently worried about Mother's constant motion—upstairs for the little ones (no downstairs nursery was ever fashioned), down into the basement for the daily wash, out into the backyard to play with the children. Going,

going, going. And she never again suffered a heart attack until a fatal one thirty-five years later.

Now I am reminded of James Michener's comments in *Sports In America*. He suggests that had the heart attack he suffered in the 1960s occurred in the 1940s, he would undoubtedly have been confined to a life of inactivity. But in the sixties, recovery called for mild exercise, gradually rebuilding the heart muscle and eventually establishing normal physical activity. In an ironic way, I now believe that Welcome House provided the exercise therapy my mother needed. In one of those strange quirks of fate, my mother may have needed the Welcome House children as badly as they needed her. Medical considerations notwithstanding, as I see it now, it was a perfect match.

Dad also had to adopt some new ways. His role as teacher and coach, of course, continued as before. With his standing in the school and community, it was natural that these brothers and sister would grow and be nurtured through the school system just as my sister and I had. The number of sons and daughters increased the responsibilities but didn't greatly alter his role, and his influence was apparent, since all of the children enjoyed their schoolwork and participated in a wide range of athletics and did extremely well. However, his summer activities clearly assumed a new pattern. Laboring in the stone quarry or guiding the Walsh children were behind him. Now he had a new family and new responsibilities. From the first year at Welcome House, a massive garden became Dad's consuming summer passion.

Eventually, he cultivated over five acres. The bounty of corn, tomatoes, beans, peppers, cabbage, cucumbers, cantaloupes, and strawberries provided a major source of food for the family. My mother, aunts (Katie Keeler and Stella Nase in particular), sister Charlotte, and others would spend many days each summer freezing or canning corn, applesauce, and other foods. Many of my friends, who often shared in the Welcome House bounty, in particular the corn (both fresh and frozen), still remember and use those vegetables as the standard for contemporary comparison, and the Welcome House vegetables always win.

It is impossible to estimate accurately the material value of this agrarian effort; however, it was considerable, since all of our summer vegetables and most of the winter vegetables were provided. Also, throughout August our typical evening meal was corn and tomatoes; and the quality was such that I never remembered hearing a complaint about repetition. Also, the strawberry season provided a main course meal of unsweetened Bisquick dough covered with milk and strawberries that everyone enjoyed. In fact, this was one of the dinners that brought in friends and relatives in large numbers.

In addition, my dad raised chickens and an occasional heifer for meat. This, I must report, became less popular as the children became attached to the animals, so it was not an annual undertaking. All in all, the garden was a major source of sustenance for the growing family. More important, I'm sure, was the activity the garden provided for a group of growing children. Here was a visual example of the work ethic and its reward; and it was a major contribution made by my father to a new family, both in nurturing the children and supporting the food budget.

Under our parents' guidance, our everyday life seemed as normal as circumstances would allow. All followed general rules of behavior, and yet no onerous rules were written or enforced. Rather, there was a natural civility that permeated our home. We knew it was wrong to "talk back" to our parents, quarrel with our brothers and sisters, neglect our school work, forget our chores, or commit any of the really serious sins (lie, steal, cheat). Occasionally some firmness was required. Our dad was a part of a "spare the rod, spoil the child" age, so in rare moments he could resort to a smack on the backside, a good shaking, but almost always a firm reprimand was all that was needed. As Bobby remembers, "He made us want to be good."

Since I was so much younger then, my tolerance may have been greater, but I never remember chaos or nasty squabbles. For example, we always had our evening meal with the entire family. We gathered around our grand table with its exciting history. In keeping with the Pearl Buck mandate and my parents' beliefs as well, the meals were hearty, nutritious, and bountiful. It was a lively but orderly hour. We discussed the day's events, school problems, or even local gossip. Little ones were not ignored, so we frequently heard about bruised knees, "naughty Paulie," or the frisky chickens that sometimes chased the kids in the backyard. Our dinners were a daily reminder of family needs, and a regular opportunity to practice our brotherly love. Unquestionably, they had a permanent, positive effect on us and were a primary source of the inner strength of Welcome House.

Birthdays and holidays were a special time for our family. We didn't celebrate birthdays with lavish parties, inviting all the classmates and friends of the celebrant. Rather, they were family times and with so many people normally around, it was easy to generate a rousing chorus of "Happy Birthday," frequently off-key. Our parents and board members provided presents. (Board members shared the responsibility of presents to prevent spoiling the children. The Biesters had Sumi, the Hammersteins had Leon, the Burpees had David, etc.) Family rules said the birthday child got to pick the menu, and fried chicken seemed to be the meal of choice. Of course, there was always a birthday cake with ice cream, and a happy time was had by all. With so many in the family, the event came up quite often. Poor Leon, with his birthday falling on December 26, seemed to have the worst time for a birthday celebration, but we managed to make the day after Christmas somehow special for him as well.

Holidays were special, too. Christmas, Easter, and New Year's were the most meaningful and the ones that varied the least from year to year. Each had family ritual within it and each had close association with church activities as well.

Easter was a time when Mother asserted her belief in a neat and tidy appearance. We could have made quite a show at the Atlantic City Easter parade had that been my parents' wish. Rather, it was Sunday morning Easter service that reviewed our Easter finery. Each child had to have a special Easter outfit and though most were made of hand-me-downs with a few special extras (a new tie, a new shirt, new shoes, or what have you), the outfit was carefully selected and specially identified as the individual's Easter outfit. Mother's impeccable side came through here, and the children went off to Easter services with great pride.

While some might see this as overemphasized materialism, there is little doubt that the children felt special, and perhaps they needed to have this type of bolstering to counteract the rejection that life tried to hand them. Easter dinner, an Easter ham with lots of mashed potatoes and vegetables, was part of the celebration, accompanied by a reminder from Dad about what the day meant. The celebration concluded with an Easter egg hunt, and the Welcome House farm was a good setting for such an activity. It also was a good time for emphasizing caring and sharing, because the older kids didn't grab all the hidden treasure. They helped the little ones get their share. The Easter holiday taught us many things.

The weeks surrounding Christmas and New Year were our happiest times. Since Dad had the school vacation all of his life, the Christmas/New Year weeks were filled with activity and freedom. Even before the little ones reached school age, they sensed special things were happening. Dad was home and great planning was always underway. Once you're exposed to the Christmas/New Year break that comes with an education schedule, it's difficult to think of Christmas and New Year's Day as one-day holidays. Everyone should have such an opportunity. The good times of these weeks certainly were important for the well-being of the Welcome House family. Common goals, the excitement of the season, joint activities—all contributed to family unity with love and spirit. It was one of the major features in making the Welcome House family so secure.

The Christmas spirit, as Dickens would contend, had an ongoing, positive effect. I agree.

In the spirit of the season, Christmas decorations became a first priority. A massive Christmas tree had to be found. The field between Welcome House and the Buck estate was covered with pines and spruces, intentionally planted by the Walshes, more for ecology than Christmas, but still a green forest with many, many selections to sort through for that perfect tree.

Normally Dad took us older boys, and whoever wanted to make the trip, into the field. Usually all the kids wanted to tag along, because this was an important decision. We preferred long needle pines; Dad liked a big, wide-based tree; Mother wanted a smaller tree that took up less room. Dad always argued (perhaps stated) that the living room was so large it didn't matter how big the tree was. Since he had the saw, we always found a large tree, and Mother always liked it. Out in the field everyone searched and everyone found the perfect tree. But we only needed one tree, not four or five. Usually, after some debate, we agreed on the tree. Frank and I dragged it home, and it found its spot in the living room next to the big upright piano. Everyone helped place the lights and ornaments in expert fashion and we all agreed it was the best tree on earth. We were easily pleased I guess, but it seemed that way to us.

The decorating continued. Each front window had a candle; twelve were needed for the three floors. Our parents chose orange lights to more closely simulate real candles, in their opinion. Some outside lights added lighting contrast and two homemade wreaths were added to our front doors (we had a front door into the kitchen and one into the living room). The decorations gave Welcome House the Christmas atmosphere, and we were ready for the day to come.

Other plans also had to be made. The meal was Mother's province. Each Christmas was just about the same—always turkey and stuffing, mashed potatoes, can-

died sweet potatoes, frozen corn (from the garden), cran-
berries, a lettuce salad with Mother's special cream dressing, and then some vegetables that varied from year to year:
string beans, lima beams, or red beets. It was a feast; it over-
loaded everyone, but all looked forward to it with great
anticipation. Mother was always pleased with the results,
and rightly so.

Presents were received, though they produced much
anxiety and suspense. Caution practiced by our parents,
and size of the family, meant that moderation must be followed. Still, our parents got presents for everyone; Gran
and Granddaddy Walsh got presents for everyone; the
Welcome House Board, using the divided system of birthday time, got presents for everyone. You can imagine the
size of the present pile with four or five presents for everyone. And this, of course, had to be planned. Telephone calls
were constant. "What do the children want?" "Do they have
enough trucks?" But it always worked out fine. We were
ready for another Christmas celebration.

For our family, Christmas began on Christmas Eve.
Our Zion Mennonite Church had a candlelight service each
year, and we always attended as a family. The service, then
and now, has carol singing and a nativity scene with church
members filling the roles of the holy family, shepherds, and
wise men. It concludes with the candle lighting ceremony.
In a darkened sanctuary, with the single Christ candle
burning by the pulpit, six junior high school girls, as
angels, light their candles from the Christ candle. Then they
slowly share the candlelight with the end person in each
pew of the congregation. The church members pass the light
to each other as the church organ and choir fill the air with
familiar Christmas music. Miraculously, the darkened
church is illuminated by the light of 400 candles as the
singing comes to an end. It is a religious experience that
never fails to bring a tear to my eye. Reminded of the
Christian message of brotherly love, I also find the shared
illumination a symbolic gesture of the church's continued
support for the Welcome House experience. Always, the

Christmas season emphasized the good spirit of Zion toward Welcome House.

The church service ended, but our Christmas Eve was far from over. At Welcome House, we adopted the system of opening presents on Christmas Eve. Our parents never emphasized the role of Santa Claus, so we didn't have to wait for him to bring the presents. Besides, they were usually spread around the tree, days ahead of Christmas, maybe because they couldn't possibly be hidden, or because Mother had to wrap them early to have them ready. At any rate, we returned from church for a snack of hot chocolate and cookies, and the eager anticipation of gift exchange. Again, the scene was not chaos. The children had great control of their emotions considering the moment. Dad usually was the "Santa," and gifts were distributed in careful order. Children were appreciative. I really don't remember any jealous rages because Leon's truck was better than mine, or what have you. It was just another example of the family functioning in a fair and rational manner. Though it may sound too good to be true, this is how it really was.

Christmas Day was a bit anti-climactic. Of course, if it fell on Sunday, we would have our regular Sunday service to attend. Otherwise, Christmas morning would be a time to play with the new toys, or reflect on the presents you received. I remember our first Christmas at Welcome House. Pearl Buck gave me a wonderful clock radio which I treasured into adulthood. She also included a generous note thanking me for helping with the new children (only Leon, David, and Sumi at that time), a note which I foolishly didn't save. Christmas dinner was generally served in the early afternoon and the menu Mother planned was executed to perfection. Like all our meals, it was a happy occasion with lively discussion and enthusiastic eating.

Clean-up was always a difficult task, because so many dishes and pots and pans were used for the feast. Mother was excused because she did the cooking. Charlotte's husband, Chuck, invariably was the dish washer, and everyone else would take turns drying the dishes. This was generally a cooperative venture, although a few always claimed to be doing the most work. I don't think it was a serious complaint, especially since Christmas Day always brought so much happiness.

And the holiday still wasn't over. We had Christmas week and another celebration to come on New Year's Day. The week between the two holidays was dedicated to good times. If the weather was cold with snow on the ground, every day there was sledding or skating. The snowmen in the yard were lots of fun; big and little kids alike joined in making the big snowballs that constituted base, body, and head. We marveled at how long these snowmen, turned into snow piles, would last into the spring thaw. As the kids grew older, the week was also a time to visit friends and relatives. All in all, these were moments that added to our memories of the good old days and helped to make us one happy family.

New Year's Day concluded the happy holidays. It, too, began for us on the evening before and, like Christmas, centered on a church service. Zion's minister, Ellis Graber, felt the New Year's celebration should be family oriented, so he organized a family night program, to be followed by a watchnight service that welcomed in the new year. The family night program usually began at nine o'clock. It was held in the Sunday school auditorium. Different church members prepared skits or songs or stories. It was really an amateur night and everyone had a good time. I particularly remember Mrs. Graber imitating a little child reciting a nursery rhyme in a forgetful and frightened manner. She was very funny. I was amazed by this because I always thought of her as serious and sedate, my notion of a typical minister's wife. Too much Nathaniel Hawthorne, I guess. At any rate, family night at Zion was a great success, and the watchnight service added another moment of reverence and meaning. Though the little ones fell asleep, everyone was excited to greet the new year.

New Year's Day was football day. Even before television, we listened to the bowl games on radio, especially the late afternoon Rose Bowl. This was important for the excited, frantic Yoder fans, and almost all of the children adopted this love of sports that Dad had. Heroes emerged— Doak Walker of SMU in the Cotton Bowl; Michigan with Bob Chappius as star halfback; a 49-0 win over California in the Rose Bowl in 1948; the supremacy of Big Ten football in this era (only one loss in the Rose Bowl during the fifties, oh, my, the inane things we remember!). We became even more committed to the football action when television came along. This could go on, but the point is, we developed a traditional day with an enjoyable activity that help offset the sad reminder that the glorious holiday season was ending. These weeks were truly happy times with great opportunities to show our feelings, to renew our commitments, and to grow in all ways. The routines we followed in those days continue for me into this time, whenever possible, and remind me so clearly of the good times our family shared.

One last holiday should be mentioned: Independence Day. Pearl Buck was frequently responsible for the way we celebrated the Fourth, and I must confess, I was almost responsible for bringing the celebration, Welcome House, or anything else that happened in the life of Pearl Buck after 1948 to an end. Let me explain this cryptic remark.

The Walshes had picnics on July Fourth whenever they were at home. They did this before and after Welcome House began, and the Yoders always were invited to these celebrations. On July 4, 1948, approximately a half year before David arrived, the Walsh picnic was in spirited progress. Good food, swimming, running races, and the like kept the Walsh children and the young guests happily entertained. The adults sat in the shade and talked, as adults are prone to do. Then Mrs. Walsh announced a surprise. Her chauffeur had brought a large box of firecrackers from the South. This was to be the highlight of the afternoon. She said twelve-year-olds could light the fireworks, if they were very careful. I know now these were illegal in Pennsylvania, but then it seemed like great fun.

All the Walsh kids, myself, and two or three other young friends took turns igniting the fuses and running away as the bombs exploded. Probably half the firecrackers were aerial bombs. These would blast the firecrackers about seventy-five to 100 feet in the air and then perform like miniature fireworks, with a loud bang and a spray of sparkling colors, even on occasion added explosions and more colors. We weren't quite up to the local fire companies' special fireworks show, but we were thrilled by the blasts and color designs, and, of course, we were the creators.

After about two-thirds of the fireworks were gone, it was my turn to light one of the larger aerial bombs. Having done this before, I apparently got a bit careless about the procedure. Our launching pad was the middle of the large Walsh yard, wide open, probably fifty feet from where the adults sat and seventy-five feet from the house and the barn.

None of the explosives fell to the earth; no trees were close by, so all the debris burned to ash before landing and threatening a fire. That is, until my turn came. I placed the bomb at the launch spot and reached toward the fuse with the burning match, but the flame burned my fingers and I jerked back, brushing the extended fuse, tipping the bomb over. Unfortunately, the match had ignited the fuse. I jumped away in horror, screaming, "Look out!" The bomb was on the ground, pointed at the startled parents. They jumped from their seats and moved to the side. The first stage of the bomb exploded, sending the aerial device hissing along the ground right past Pearl Buck's now vacated chair. The device continued across the stone patio, collided with the wall of the house behind the parents, rebounded into the air, and exploded with a loud bang. Bright flashes and other bombs cascaded off chairs, tables, and shrubs. It was a spectacular scene, but no one appreciated it, least of all me.

The cook came running out to see what all the commotion was about, but once the bomb burned out, there was no commotion. There was deadly silence. I, of course, was as embarrassed as a twelve-year-old could be and could only say what a twelve-year-old could say.

Near tears, I stammered, "I don't know what happened, I'm sorry."

Kindly, one of the Walshes responded. I was too upset to remember who said it, but it was something like, "It's all right, no one was hurt. Let's put the rest of the fireworks away."

Thank goodness for that. The thought of serious injury to anyone there gives me a chill even today. The rest of the day has faded from my memory, for obvious reasons, I suppose.

The results of this day could be mentioned. First, my blunder didn't prevent Pearl Buck from selecting our family to be the Welcome House family or telling my parents I was the best little boy she knew. Secondly, my action seemed to be an early start toward a lifetime of clumsy blunders. Thirdly, though we had other July Fourth picnics, we never had fireworks again.

The above examples of Welcome House life support the conclusion that the family did not succumb to the potential obstacle that ethnic differences represented in those years, but rather that the family existed as a happy, well-functioning unit. Also a number of anecdotes, serving as momentary glimpses rather than repeated patterns, further explain why the Welcome House plan worked.

Pearl Buck apparently believed this, promoting such sentiment with an anecdote she told frequently, explaining that the event she witnessed convinced her that her Welcome House dream would succeed. It all happened in the third year of Welcome House. The setting was Charlotte's wedding ceremony. David and Mother were the key players in the scene. David, as ring bearer in the wedding, was a bit young to grasp his function (he was only three and one-half at the time) and was obviously frightened as his turn came to walk down the aisle. He panicked and refused to move. Finally, one of the bridesmaids had to lead him through the processional, and when he reached the front of the sanctuary, he stopped and literally shook with fear.

Pearl Buck always relished the next moment, for as she described, "Mother's strong arm reached over the front pew and plucked the frightened child from his plight." For her, this spontaneous act was proof of Mother's ability to protect her children and keep them safe and sheltered. This rather simple but dramatic act stood as testimony for Pearl Buck that the Yoders could handle the difficulties of raising the Welcome House children. Perhaps this is overstating the event, but the mother-child interaction was truly a most poignant moment and all who witnessed it would agree. Mother rescued David with an instinctive reaction to his crisis. Our parents invariably found satisfactory solutions when faced with family predicaments. Most were typical of any parent-child interactions: the denied request for candy, the bruised knee, the child's wish to stay up later than usual, the special need for personal belongings like clothing or sporting goods, and the like. With so many children and so many possible requests and/or conflicts, it would seem likely that constant turmoil would be a reality. But that isn't the way it was.

How was the turmoil averted? Was there a planned strategy carefully worked out by our parents? Probably not. Rather, my dad's successful teaching experience and my mother's natural ability as a parent were the proper ingredients to keep family difficulties to a minimum. By their efforts, life was under control.

Another early family moment adds more. My mother told this story on numerous occasions, so I remember it well even though I wasn't present when it happened. A Saturday shopping trip to Philadelphia with the five little ones served as the setting. We older children remained at home doing our chores and our own activities. This excursion is a good example of how well the family was functioning. Taking five small children into the big city reveals the type of parental control my parents wielded and the good behavior the little ones exhibited, but there is more to this story.

A popular part of the trip was lunch in the dining room of Gimbel's Department Store, always promoted by Mother as a major reward for good children. Seated in the dining room and waiting for my dad, who had rushed off to check on a forgotten purchase, my mother, as she later reported, witnessed the numerous subtle and not-so-subtle glances that were directed her way as all the little ones babbled away and, of course, called her "Mother." An obviously international group of children with an obviously American mother was a tantalizing subject for inquisitive minds, or, less kindly put, busybodies. When an obviously American "Daddy" joined the table minutes later, it was too much. Jaws dropped; perplexity reigned. Remember, these were the early fifties. The meaning and lesson of this story, however, comes from my parents, who were not angered by such rudeness. They understood why people would be curious, and they tolerated their curiosity. What they really hoped for was to have everyone match their own feelings. While others saw children with different skin color or Asian features, my parents saw only children. And they loved them without condition.

Further anecdotal evidence adds considerably to the notion that Welcome House was on the right track. Many happened throughout the years as my brothers and sisters grew and became active in the community at large. However, a few more examples complete the picture of a stable and thriving early Welcome House. One concerns Frank and his aforementioned enterprising spirit.

Among the many money-making operations that Frank developed was a part-time job working early mornings for the farmer that directed the Pearl Buck agricultural operation. Basically, Frank helped in the dairy, both milking the cows and cleaning the cow stalls. It was hard work at an awful hour, but it served as a way for Frank to continue his ever-present desire to succeed.

In mid-December of his second year at Welcome House, Frank came up with a generous idea. He wanted to give Mr. Akers, the farm foreman, a surprise present. Frank thought that on Christmas day he could recruit some helpers and complete the chores by the time that Mr. Akers arrived to do the work. Johnny Walsh, one of Pearl Buck's sons, was also working for the dairy at that time, so Frank and Johnny and two sleepy recruits, brother Ray and myself, trudged to the dairy barn on a cold December morning an hour and a half before the usual starting time. Frank directed, and within the time period, we completed the milking and the clean-up. Then we waited for the moment when Mr. Akers would arrive. It was a happy moment with the anticipated result. Mr. Akers was touched, appreciative, and almost speechless. We were all happy with our effort, although it proved to me that five a.m. was not a proper time for earning one's living. Frank's thoughtfulness captured the Welcome House spirit. He was sharing what he learned at home. His thoughtful and unique gift gave joy to all who participated, recipient and givers alike. And there is an interesting continuation.

Two years later, in *Women's Home Companion*, a short story appeared entitled "The Christmas Gift." The author was Pearl Buck. In the story, a young farm boy agonized over his inability to buy his father a proper Christmas gift because he had no money. Searching for a solution to his personal crisis, the youth hit upon an idea. On Christmas Day, he would arise early and do all the farm chores. The scene was played out to a happy climax—a proud father, a happy son, a best gift ever. Pearl Buck, of course, had been told of Frank's gift. Like many good writers, she found real life served her well and the gift of that Christmas morning, 1951, remains forever in printed lore of American short stories. The spirit of Welcome House lives on in yet another way.

Pearl Buck was a constant part of our lives through these years. She came to Welcome House every week, often two or three times a week when she wasn't traveling. Whenever she came, she joined in whatever was needed for the children: bathing, feeding, diapering. Sometimes she would read to them or tell a story of old China. She was not the celebrity here; she was the grandmother in action. Her contributions were vital to the children. She brought wisdom, experience, and an international perspective to an international family. Though everyone loved and respected her, she sometimes demonstrated to us older, "wiser" children that innate brilliance did not always convert into everyday common sense. An anecdote serves this conclusion.

On a Saturday morning in late fall of 1951, a phone call came from Gran Walsh. She wanted to bring some visitors to meet the family that afternoon. Of course, my parents were eager to have everything most presentable, so work assignments were quickly handed out. As a sign of the times, gender roles prevailed, so the females had to take care of the housecleaning, while we older brothers were given garden and lawn duty. Welcome House trees were abundant, dropping tons of leaves each fall. Most of the fall leaves must have been waiting for us that day because we worked up a good set of blisters, raking all morning. By noontime Ray, Frank, and I had removed every last one of those leaves from the front and side yards. A careful sweeping of the terrace and walkways gave us a garden that we felt compared favorably to any place on earth. Wearily we surveyed our handiwork. For me, then and now, the scene before us, our Welcome House garden, had an Edenic quality.

Remembering that scene evokes nostalgic images and they remain clear, withstanding the dimming effects of time. The massive maple tree in the front lawn, a tree taller than our three-and-one-half-story house, with a trunk too large in circumference to reach around, and telephone pole spikes hammered into it by an unknown previous occupant, ideal for aiding a climb to heights that frightened even the climber; a massive willow tree in the backyard that later succumbed to a heavy windstorm, but fortunately fell away from the house, for it would have done serious damage even to our stone fortress had it come our way; a wonderful apple tree with branches that provided a good substitute for a jungle gym and sweet fruit that was a fair substitute for a Hershey bar; a stand of blueberry bushes that yielded many buckets of berries which, thankfully, the little kids loved to pick; a three-board white fence that surrounded our entire vegetable garden and added to the feeling of security within; a stone terrace encircled by flowers and a foot-high picket fence, carefully and lovingly constructed by Dad with his children's support.

That morning was a moment in time, a kind of snapshot of history that will never leave me. The visual splendor, the implied security, the recognized purpose of Welcome House, all meshed to clarify in my young mind what my parents were doing. It was a defining experience for me and I remember it so very clearly. Was it a Garden of Eden? But I digress. Inside everything had passed Mother's careful inspection, so we all breathed easily and waited for Gran and her guests (some potential Welcome House donors).

Mrs. Walsh, as always, entered smiling. As she introduced everyone, she commented on how splendid everything looked. She went on to say, "It certainly is good fortune that the fall winds arrived and blew every last leaf from your front lawn." Frank and I gave each other knowing glances. Ray, being younger, began to protest, but we silenced him. Later we agreed, here again was proof that brilliance and common sense weren't always partners. I suppose in our own immature minds we were finding a way to be comfortable in the presence of greatness. We also thought we were quite generous because we forgave her for her mistakes. Such is youth.

At Welcome House, the older children had a very positive influence on the little ones. Serving as role models, helping with all family needs from diapering to baby-sitting, showing love and respect, all contributed to the sanctity, security, and happiness of the home, and my parents appreciated the effort. This was generally, though not always, true. One particularly embarrassing example revealed the occasional breakdown.

When I reached sixteen years, I, like all my peers, eagerly earned my driver's license. This badge of independence made me a particular hero with the little Yoders, for now I could drive the children to nursery school (as they came of age), to their sister Charlotte's home to play with Jenny Lou or Mary Jean, or on special outings (to the store for ice cream, a ball game, etc.). One day I took David, then about four and a half, to a local fair. Arriving at the fair, I immediately struck up a conversation with some friends. David drifted off to watch one of the energetic and animated barkers trying to sell his wares. In the meantime, I wandered back to the car and left the parking lot. In a moment of terror I realized that I had forgotten David. I retraced my steps as quickly as I have ever done anything in my life, to find the abandoned child with a family friend, looking sadly and searchingly for his missing older brother. A few well-chosen and accurate words of admonishment from our family friend only added to my embarrassment. We hurried away, David with reduced respect for his older brother, I'm sure, I with a greater awareness of the responsibility necessary to take care of our younger siblings.

In truth, this is one of the few examples of irresponsibility that occurred during the child-rearing years. Charlotte, from her vantage point as older sister, and with her initial position as Mother's helper, and later pinch-hitter for all emergency chores, was particularly good at aiding in the training and control of the growing babies. Even today, she holds the position of family arbitrator or confidant, since she managed to win the respect and loyalty of all the children through the early times.

Frank was also a formidable figure to the younger children. As would be expected, he was particularly concerned about his biological brother and sister, Ray and Lillian, and with his innate personal standards, insisted they emulate him since he was so dedicated and goal-oriented. Frank also commanded respect from Bobby during Bobby's days of adjustment to the Welcome House scene. Bobby remembers a specific time when Frank taught him some proper behavior after one of Bobby's "naughty" acts.

It seems Bobby had been given a cherry bomb by one of his school friends one day. He thought he would have some fun so he lit the bomb and rolled it into Frank's room. The explosion frightened Frank. He only realized what had happened when he discovered a laughing Bobby outside his door. Quite angry, he made Bobby stand with arms outstretched and books on each hand as a punishment. Bobby accepted Frank's punishment and was determined to hold the books until Frank excused him, but he remembers his perseverance finally collapsed and the books likewise. Frank asked him whether he had learned his lesson. He confessed he had, and asked that Frank not "tell on him." Frank agreed and so a kind of big brother-little brother treaty added considerably to the mutual respect they had for each other. The years were regularly filled with similar interactions.

By way of contrast, I had a less pleasant experience that nevertheless had a positive result, since Paul and myself, the two siblings involved, learned a great deal from it. During these years Paul was always the most active of the children, to put it kindly. More specifically, he was the naughtiest, but it was born of an outgoing and mischievous personality that was full of spirit and happiness. One day Paul was being disciplined for one of his regular mistakes, so he was grounded and couldn't make a Saturday afternoon trip to a local store. I was the only other person at home, so I was assigned the role of "jailer," keeping Paul in the house and out of trouble. This was impossible at best.

After some disagreement Paul, who was about six at the time, announced he was going outside. I said that was not allowed by the terms of his punishment. He went anyway. I chased after him and he climbed on top of our spring house, a building with a roof that was close to the ground at one end and sloped upward to about seven feet at the other end. Paul stood on top of the roof at the high end. I was on the ground looking up and telling him to come down and go in the house where he belonged.

"No," he said.

"Yes," I said.

But the six-year-old won, because within the next few seconds, he was doing a perfect imitation of the famous Belgian statue, *Mannequin Pis*, only instead of the concrete receiving pool, he had me. Fortunately, the shoppers returned at this moment, so the only reaction was Paul being marched off for one more of his many punishments and me scurrying off for a very necessary shower. The rest of the children knowingly talking about "that naughty Paul" and me muttering about responsibilities of older brotherhood, concluded the event. Ah, the vicissitudes of life!

How many stories are needed to capture the happy family in this most unusual social setting? The years were filled with them, of course. What I've shared up to this time is drawn from memory and experience. Another source, and one that exists because of Pearl Buck's educational interests, was the *Green Hills News*.

The *Green Hills News* was a mimeographed collection of the Walsh family activities. The paper included editorial comments, family announcements, vacation memories, children's activities, and adult commentary. Through the early fifties, the twenty-five-page paper was published about three times per year. Originally, it carried the motto "A Family Newspaper For the Information and Interest Of Our Family." September 1952, the paper stated "A Family Newspaper For the Information and Interest Of Our Family and the Welcome House Families." In 1953, "and Friends" was added to the motto.

The *Green Hills News* documents much about the life and values of the Walsh family in these years. It also offers some glimpses into the life at Welcome House. In general, the paper revealed the early training the Walshes impressed upon their children to read, reflect, and write. A thirteen-year-old Edgar, in an editorial of July 1951, critically assessed the "world adults are placing on the youth of America."

"Certain people stand out," he wrote. "Ghandi, Rufus Jones, Madame Pandit, and Pearl Buck. . . . They see the world as it is, and as it could be, and they are willing to work to make the two come together." Not all the articles rested on such worldly concerns. New pets, summer plans, or good books were also discussed. And, in all editions, some attention was paid to the life at Welcome House. The children contributed frequently. (Lillian's school trip to the State Capital is found in the July 1951 issue.) Pearl Buck regularly described some aspect of Welcome House, from fundraising to children's anecdotes; Dad regularly wrote a short column on the happenings at home. What is captured in those pages is very revealing.

Some of the words of Pearl Buck seem appropriate to include here. These first comments are her early assessment of the children as they began their first years at Welcome House. They were written in the summer of 1951:

Our children are all doing well and giving us much pleasure and interest. To begin with the oldest: Frank is working this summer at a regular job with Fischer and Porter, the precision tool company. Kermit Fischer, its president, is the treasurer of Welcome House and his keen interest and constant help are indispensable. Dale Yoder has a job there, too, and Kermit reports that both boys are working well and are making friends among the other men.

Lillian has been taking music lessons all year and is learning to help her mother, Mrs. Yoder, and to become an expert with babies and in being a big sister. She and Jean have made a sisterhood of their own. Lillian has a new dog which she faithfully calls a collie. The rest of us are still being polite, but we are thinking thoughts about collies and what they are and are not.

Ray is going to camp this summer. He has a full scholarship at Camp Pocono and we are sure he will have a good time, though we shall miss his two big black eyes and his quick smile. Mrs. Fischer is taking him to the camp with her son Jimmy on the same trip.

Bobby Lee comes next in age and when we think of the boy who came to us just before Christmas and the boy we have now, we are grateful to all the family at Welcome House, but especially the parents, for the immense improvement. Bobby will go to camp next summer if he likes, but this summer he is still in need of the family atmosphere.

David, our brown-eyed poet, is growing tall and handsome. He has been at nursery school all year and gained very much from the experience. He will be four in September but he seems much older than his age. When he wants to be big he plays with Bobbie Lee. When he feels little he plays with Leon and Sumie.

Leon and Sumie are still our almost-twins, though when Leon does not want Sumie to take turns with the tractor he explains to her very carefully, "You too little, Sumie, you too, too little." He takes turns nicely with David, with occasional relapses, and they are devoted to each other. Leon talks very well now. He was two years old last December but he is big for his age.

Sumie is still tiny, weighing less than Jackie. But she is plump and well, and she talks, too. She is not a chatterbox as Leon is, and when she says something it is important and we all listen. She is so pretty and so small that she is a delight to dress up in little short pink frocks and brimmed bonnets, a pocket-sized lady if there ever was one, very precise, very neat with her tiny fingers, quick to notice anything decorative in the way of dress. She will be an artist of some sort, in miniature. She is a little mother to the three small boys.

Jackie, now fourteen months old, runs everywhere, says a few words, is always ready to eat, is very big for his age, has a wonderful disposition and now and then, when he feels outraged, a terrific temper. He considers himself the equal of anybody and such is his natural air of the aristocrat that he would, we feel sure, treat King George himself with the manner of an equal. He likes to be left alone to work out his

own plans, but now and then at the end of a long busy day
when he has accomplished a great deal, he likes to forget that
he is grown up and much occupied with affairs of state.
Then he wants to sit on some comfortable lap, his mother's
always preferred, although his Gran's will do if his mother
is not around, and be cuddled for a bit.

One year later, when Paul became part of the family, she
wrote:

> *He is of the same background as David Yoder, but he is*
> *only two years old. Mr. and Mrs. Yoder would not hear of*
> *his going anywhere else except to them, and in as much as it*
> *is improbable that offers for adoption will be made for him,*
> *he is with the Yoders. Though very tiny, Paul is an adven-*
> *turer, extremely articulate and a leader in every activity.*
> *He instigates unexpected behavior in the heretofore digni-*
> *fied and rather correct child, Jackie, and leads him on*
> *expeditions which fill their mother with horror. "Where is*
> *Paul?" is now the Yoder slogan. Meanwhile Jackie, who is*
> *one of those strong silent men by nature, has been compelled*
> *to increase his vocabulary rather quickly in order to cope*
> *with Paul, to whom he spends a great deal of time saying,*
> *"No, no, Paulie," without visible effect.*

We welcome all these children with love.

A few family anecdotes make their way into print.
Sumie and Leon seem to attract the most attention. Leon's
reaction to the family dog rolling on the grass is recorded.
"Oh look, Prince is fighting all by himself." His favorite
food also provides some humor. "Please give me some more
rackamoni—I love rackamoni." Sumie (her name was
spelled Sumie until she began school) had an interesting
encounter with one of our barnyard inhabitants. Pearl
Buck described it in this fashion:

> *Sumie is small and the hen is big. The hen had*
> *hatched a whole flock of little bantam chicks, and she fussed*
> *over them all the time. But our Sumie, who cannot resist the*
> *miniature, could not refrain from trying to pick up one of*

the chicks, in spite of previous warnings. What horror! The red hen flew at Sumie. Mr. Yoder, peacefully cultivating his vegetable patch, looked up to see the usually sedate Sumie, racing across the lawn, screaming for her life. Twice the red hen pecked Sumie on the fat little thigh before her father could rescue her from the frightful fowl. For days thereafter, long after the traces of the pecks had disappeared, Sumie would, upon request, lift her four inches or so of skirt and point to a spot upon her plump hip, at first real but afterwards imaginary, and she would say with profound gravity, "Hen pecked me here," raising large black eyes to the inquirer's sympathetic face.

I have two brief comments on this tale. Today Sumi disputes the accuracy of the account, though I believe her quarrel is with adjectives used to describe thigh and hip, not that the aggressive mother hen ever chased her across the backyard. And second, there seemed to be a rather regular presence of this type of fowl in the Welcome House barnyard. A large rooster, formerly one of those baby chicks, cruelly colored at Easter time in an age before such practices were condemned, somehow survived and decided he was king of the backyard. Perhaps his origins had made him particularly nasty. At any rate, he refused to allow Mother to hang out her laundry, regularly chasing her back into the house. Although the aggressive mother hen was tolerated because her little chicks needed her, the Easter rooster had overstepped his authority. Dad told the family that the rooster, like other "nasty" chickens that preceded him, "had run away." The family accepted this explanation. My own feeling was that he was using the wrong verb.

Dad's contribution to the *Green Hills News* offered details on the family. The summer of 1954, while Frank, Lillian, Ray, and I were all working and away from home throughout the day, found the young children involved in the following:

Our first project was to build a terrace in the back of our house and a small terrace on the side of the front porch. Everyone wanted to be helpful, so each was given a job.

Paul's job was to supply the water in mixing the concrete by turning on and off the spigot. This was fun, particularly if he could turn it on at the wrong time. Jackie held the trowel and tried to use it now and then. David and Bobby Lee used a hoe to mix the stones, sand, and cement, and Paul's water. You've guessed it. . . .

Leon was the general supervisor. The stones were gathered in the fields. All in all, it was a lot of fun.

Dad also reported building picnic tables and benches "since the children liked to eat outside." They enjoyed this effort, "for when do you find a youngster who does not like to hammer?" They also painted their handiwork. As Dad wrote, "When the job was finished, you could take one look at any of them and you were certain that everything was painted green."

But what a thrill the accomplishment must have been. And it should be remembered that the work crew consisted of one eight-year-old, one five-year-old, one four-year-old, and two three-year-olds. There is a message here, and I think it is obvious.

Throughout these columns, both from the Walshes and from my dad, there is the constant repetition of optimism and constant indication of good spirit and joy. My dad regularly shared his feelings. "We want to express our appreciation to all who have been so kind and generous to all of us," from August 1954. Similar comments are found in statements from other issues.

Pearl Buck wrote about Bobby Lee:

If ever we doubted the wisdom of Welcome House, and we never do, Bobby Lee would be the answer. When he came to us last Christmas, so short a time ago, and to see our boy now, we know that Welcome House is right. There is a joy in seeing our children grow and develop and overcome the difficulties of other years, and we wish that everyone who reads this could understand and share the joy. It enriches life, and we are sorry for anyone who is without it.

And finally she wrote,

> These are our own children, all interesting, all valuable
> and lovable. They have faults, I suppose, but I have never
> been able to notice them.

These words are echoed through the years. Certainly Mother and Dad believed them; my sister and I believed them; and as I hope to demonstrate, the community, school, and church believed them. Now it is time to take the Welcome House story into the outside world. The following will reveal how Welcome House members existed within, and were supported in, three major areas: church, school, and community. It is as I contend and indicated earlier, the successful involvement with these three that makes the Welcome House experiment work. Here is the evidence.

Our family with Dad and Mother (Lloyd and Viola Yoder) at Welcome House in 1953; (back, left to right): Dale, Lillian, and Frank; (middle): Bobby Paul, Mother, Jack, Dad, Sumi, and Ray; (front): David and Leon; Scott and Charlotte are missing.

The Yoder chldren in 1984: (standing, left to right): Sumi, Scott, Lillian, Dale. Charlotte, Ray and Frank; (kneeling): Leon, David, and Paul; Bobby and Jack are missing.

Viola Yoder, the mother of Welcome House, "has fun" with David (left) and Leon, two of the children.

Healthy, boisterous children play in the front yard of our home under Mother's watchful eye at Welcome House.

Pearl Buck, Mrs. Richard Walsh in private life, reading a story to the Yoder children at Welcome House. The novelist and her husband considered themselves too old to adopt children when they started the home to care for Asian-American children.

My brother, David Yoder, holds a play telephone for Pearl Buck.

David takes delight in lighting the pipe of Richard J. Walsh, who with his wife, Pearl Buck, was a moving spirit behind Welcome House.

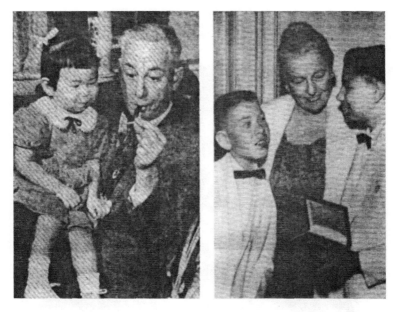

Left: My sister, Sumie Mishima Yoder (three), blows out the matches for our "Granddaddy" Richard Walsh. Right: Pearl S. Buck receives a locket from Leon Yoder (left) and David Yoder (right) at a Bellevue-Stratford Hotel dinner.

— *Chapter 6* —

THE WELCOME HOUSE FAMILY MEETS THE WORLD OUTSIDE

For the Welcome House family, our home was the hub of life. Mother and the small children, in particular, spent almost all of their days on our fifteen-acre farm. True, there were occasional visits to the Walshes, even less frequent visits to friends and relatives, an annual shopping trip with Mother and Dad, a very occasional dinner at Goldies Diner in Dublin (once every two months or so), Sunday morning church, and that just about covers the regular away-from-home activities of Mother and the little Yoders. This was not a depressing existence, as we have seen. In most ways it was just the opposite. But it was quite isolated, and one might raise some legitimate questions about the isolation. Could it make our "different" children feel even more different from their contemporaries? Will they be sufficiently socialized at school age to join the student body without consequence? Will they know enough about the world away from Welcome House? Could the isolation become a reason for Welcome House failure?

Not to worry is how one comedian might answer such queries. First, if the family was too large to be entertained by friends in the community, let's bring the community to them. As a consequence, the Yoders did a great deal of entertaining. Large dinner parties (the aforementioned strawberry shortcake feasts are an example), summer picnics with friends and relatives, special functions such as the annual Men's Sunday School breakfast, or the end-of-the-year picnic for the entire faculty of Dad's school, visits from friends with small children, close friends playing cards, particularly in the snowy winters around the cozy fire in our den, summertime ball games—these and other activities made for an active Welcome House social calendar.

The children were always involved with these social events. They got to know people and people came to know them. This was far from isolation, and the children were simply children. It was natural and it was integrating, and their so-called differences were meaningless. The local community came to Welcome House by our parents' invitation, and this, in my opinion, helped to normalize the life experiences of unusual, partially isolated children. Amazingly, the world community came to Welcome House by Pearl Buck's invitation, and this provided experiences that few have had. Undoubtedly, the children were learning many things from people of national and international fame. What a positive blessing this was. And it was happening in a small, rural community whose people would rarely venture beyond the local terrain, for whom a trip to Philadelphia or a vacation to Atlantic City was a major effort, only undertaken after long planning.

And into this environment came the friends of Pearl Buck. One day the Dalai Lama of Tibet arrived and spent the greater part of an afternoon in our living room, speaking, praying, and playing with two-year-old Leon. Prime Minister Nehru of India also was a dignitary from afar who came to visit the international family. His picture, taken with three-year-old David, remains part of the family history and is often shared as an important moment in our past. American celebrities were frequently welcomed. Whenever the person was well-known, there was a great deal of gawking and chattering by the older children.

A very definite Broadway connection had been cultivated by Pearl Buck. The Hammerstein and Rodgers team is a key example. They received special adulation from the older children because they were so well-known and visited quite often. And, of course, they were factors in the Welcome House success story. Through them, the musical comedy genre was opened to the rural world of Welcome House. Shirley Jones, Gordon MacCrea, and Mary Martin were all featured stars who, in turn, became friends of Welcome House. My mother was particularly fond of the talented Shirley Jones, and after they met she was even more impressed with her as a person. Billy Rose of Golden Horseshoe fame and Eleanor Holme were New Yorkers who came to Bucks County on more than one occasion and were always kind and wonderful to the little children. It is difficult to calculate the exact impact these people had on Welcome House, but it had to be considerable.

There were a few occasions when our parents were invited to New York. Thus a number of celebrity connections were also made on the Great White Way. Family members recall our parents speaking of meeting such stars as Eleanor Parker, Helen Hayes, and Jimmy Stewart. Later, Dorothy Kilgallen took part in special fundraising. James Michener, already connected to Welcome House through his board membership, added further prestige to the assembled friends of Welcome House with his literary excellence and his international fame. All the famous people brought special ideas and a degree of sophistication to our Welcome House life.

Welcome House was also promoted through national coverage. Much of that promotion came through Pearl Buck, frequently on television talk shows discussing her latest book, but always including Welcome House and the plight of unwanted children as a major emphasis of her interview. Dennis James, a Philadelphia television personality (she later reported how embarrassed she was when he kissed her on the cheek in show biz style), and Edward R. Murrow on his popular Person to Person television show, are examples. It was exciting to see Pearl Buck on television. The person who was Grandmother to the family, who came to our door on a regular basis, was on the set in our den. It was magical and memorable because during the early fifties, television became an active part of our lives.

Ironically, one of the early means of contact with the world outside our home was that technological marvel. I say ironic because television seemed to lessen outside contact by physically holding people in the confines of their television rooms. Witness the early years of the television world. Movie attendance dropped; restaurants tried to lure people away from TV dinners with specials and altered schedules; service clubs accommodated its members by dropping Tuesday night meetings, the night of the very popular Milton Berle and his Texaco Hour. Yet while keeping people home, it also brought sights and sounds from the outside world, never before possible. Far from sophisticated and often fantasy, still television introduced news, music, drama, individual personalities (faces, no longer just voices), movies, and the like in ways that were never before experienced.

For our family, with its stay-at-home lifestyle, this was a magic carpet flight taking us anywhere. We embraced television as a welcome intruder. Though a wasteland in some eyes, television helped us discover there were many things outside our isolation, and for that reason, it was good. Also, television was an entertaining companion for Mother during the many nights her husband and older children had church or school activities. One final irony, the Mennonite culture originally resisted television, judging it to be a temptation with evil consequences. But our Church Conference had no restrictions so we joined the television culture and spent a great many family hours within the TV glow.

Some information on television history might explain why television could catch our family's attention so fully. We were like so many others in the late forties and early fifties when the television phenomenon began. It was so new and so different. And most important, I think, it was so easy. Turn the knob and your favorite stars were in your living room. At its inception, however, few envisioned its future growth and impact. Originating in the 1920s, television could only produce blurry on-screen images, with no general public use. However, various events reached limited receivers throughout the 1930s and 1940s: the Presidential election in 1932, a Gertrude Lawrence play in 1938, a college baseball game in 1938, the Republican convention in 1940, Brooklyn Dodgers baseball in 1941, V.E. Day celebration in 1945.

Immediate visual access to newsworthy action made some believe that a new age was coming. More, however, scoffed. Television was judged a fad with a limited future. We know now who was correct. By 1947, 14,000 homes were receiving the first regular programs. Kraft Theater; Meet the Press; Kukla, Fran and Ollie; and Howdy Doody were the most noteworthy entries in this year, and the World Series was telecast for all set owners for the first time. The television years were underway. The influence was immediate, electing politicians, creating stars and celebrities, and altering all sorts of social habits. Cable networks and VCR's make almost any event available to the viewer. Americans average almost twenty hours per week in front of the screen, and over 92,000,000 television sets are currently in use. No longer do we speak of the fad with a limited future. And we were there. We felt the changes television brought to American life.

Our community, and in turn, individual families, addressed the television age in a rather unique way. The "Old Mennonites" with their plain ways did not allow movie attendance as part of their members' lives. Television was in this interpretation, an in-house movie, and thus disallowed. Our General Conference had no restrictions on movie attendance. It was one of the distinctions frequently made between the "old" and "new" congregations. So if one could afford the new gadget, a "new Mennonite" could have it, but the community felt other pressures. Certain of the "old Mennonites" were showing restlessness with some of the church's rejections of modern life. Television seems to have been the proverbial straw that broke the camel's back. A group split from the Blooming Glen church and established a new, thriving congregation five miles from

town. Perjoratively referred to as the "television Mennonites," this group adopted middle ground between the existing Mennonite churches. Some hard feelings resulted, but
soon dissipated. Eventually the "old Mennonite" recanted
on television restrictions and many in the church purchased
sets. The television age had arrived and everywhere people
felt its influence. Blooming Glen was no exception. And as
we shall see, neither was Welcome House.

We owned no television before Welcome House,
though we were affected by the growing television culture.
I was first introduced to the magical medium in the mid-
forties. My father's good friend was the son of a very successful meat packer, Charles Fehl, one of Blooming Glen's
aforementioned businesses. The Fehl family had one of the
few television receivers in the entire county in those days,
and, of course, programming was extremely limited. But a
regular Saturday afternoon offering was the U.S. Military
Academy football games. My dad and I were regular view-
ers on these Saturday afternoons, and Glenn Davis and Doc
Blanchard, the touchdown twins of those great Army teams,
became my special heroes. The hoopla of West Point and
its football program mesmerized a little rural nine-year-old.
Television transported me to a place I had never been to
see things I had never known. It was the beginning of my
understanding of "television travel." I was fascinated and
I guess hooked. Later in the forties our friends the
Spanningers and the Moyers purchased television sets. With
my young friends, we saw the daring action of afternoon
cowboys (Hopalong Cassidy, Tom Mix, Ted Steele, or
Buster Crabbe). We laughed at the nighttime stars, Milton
Berle, Arthur Godfrey, and Henry Aldrich. It was not intellectual growth, but I learned things I would not have
known. The TV took us to many places. It was from my
own experience that I realize the role television had on the
Welcome House family.

Our first Welcome House years continued without
our personal television. But in the spring of 1951, an anony-
mous donor made our family very happy. A table model

Muntz TV arrived at our door and our lives changed. This was not a big luxury set, but it delivered all the programs just the same. All the family developed TV habits. The little ones loved the Howdy Doody, Buffalo Bob genre. Though Mother placed some limits on their television time, they had regular morning programs that they watched with glee. Dad and the older children were most attracted to the sports programs. The Gillette boxing matches (which Mother hated), football, baseball, and basketball games were all major attractions.

We had the good fortune (I think) to have an ideal television location at Welcome House. Our hillside captured the regular television signal from Philadelphia, plus a clear signal from many New York stations. As a consequence, we were treated to the successful New York Knickerbockers, professional basketball champions of the early fifties. Carl Braun, Ernie Vanderweighe, Dick McGuire, Harry "the Horse" Gallatin became another set of sports heroes for me. The New York channels also brought some of the New York City culture into our home, another example of the outside world coming into our lives.

My mother loved the earlier situation comedies, in particular "I Love Lucy" and "My Little Margie." Television served as a major entertainment outlet for our mother, because she was tied to the house during the early years of Welcome House. My dad's many responsibilities in school, church, and community took him away from home regularly throughout the week, so Mother used the TV as her personal escape. There are a few strange anomalies to report, and I have no definitive answer to the puzzle to this day.

One night a young Johnny Carson popped up as an unexpected comedy half-hour, and my mother laughed and enjoyed the show like few others. He was Mother's favorite throughout her life. Often Mother could be quite negative about deficiencies she perceived in someone's personal life. For instance, Johnny Carson's marital record would seemingly cause her great concern. For some reason, she accepted his life and made him one of her celebrity heroes. No amount of teasing or no charge of inconsistency could shake her conviction on the merit of Carson. Another unexplainable television alliance was with professional wrestling, in sharp contrast to her view of boxing. Here the debate became even more forceful. Mother believed that the contests were real, and she would argue heatedly that we didn't know what we were talking about. Don Eagle, of the hair style fame, was her favorite. His athleticism was an obvious truth and his acrobatic tricks were undeniable, but the results were clearly preordained. So strong was her interest that I remember braving an ice storm to visit our former neighbors, the Ralph Moyers in Blooming Glen, to see a Don Eagle match during the days before we had our own television. Such was the puzzle, and while her sense of fairness and perhaps forgiveness in the Carson case was an indication of her generosity, the attraction to wrestling just defies explanation. Perhaps she was just putting us on and she was playing a gigantic hoax. I wish I could ask her now.

One final note: there were family moments that surrounded the television life that are worth recalling. We all liked to end the week with the Sunday night program, "What's my Line?" By today's standards, it is a low-cost show, perhaps, too pretentious. For those who don't remember, the show had four panelists who tried to guess the occupation of a guest. Dorothy Kilgallen, Bennet Cerf, Arlene Francis, and a guest panelist asked questions, and host John Daly guided the guests until the occupation was identified or the panel received ten negative responses to its questions. For us, the program served as a nice capstone to the normally busy and sometimes frantic weekend, and paved the way for the new week ahead. Frequently we were joined by family friends, the Elvin Souders. I remember fun being poked at Dorothy Kilgallen. She seemed stiff and humorless. By contrast, everyone enjoyed Arlene Francis and host John Daly. It was always a fun-filled family moment, just good, lighthearted entertainment. And it was a family ritual.

In conclusion, the television in our den, contrary to its reputation as a technological invader that destroyed family life, seemed to have the opposite effect. Note, it was not an all-consuming passion for us, but when the TV was on, it was a family activity. Furthermore, we adopted an interesting convention that reveals the respect we had for each other. For those moments when nearly all of us assembled for a show (Milton Berle, Martin and Lewis on the Colgate Hour, Arthur Godfrey), we followed a rule that is still occasionally rolled out when we gather for family functions. If anyone had to leave the den for bathroom, snack, telephone, or the like, a simple declaration, "seat saved," did just that. No one shifted to the better seat just vacated. Thus television was a part of the growing family. Its use was one more example of Welcome House in the changing times of the 1950s, and more importantly, it gave us another lifeline to the world around us. I'm happy it wasn't the only one, but it served a purpose.

The annual summer vacation was an opportunity for the little ones to experience life from beyond our fifteen acres. It also strengthened the family unit through new and often exciting experiences. Like all of our activities, everyone eagerly awaited our summer excursions. For the first two years of Welcome House, our vacation was at Island Beach, New Jersey, just south of Seaside Heights. The island, owned by the federal government, had once been a Coast Guard station. Throughout the late 1940s and 1950s, the abandoned Coast Guard houses were rented to people as vacation sites. Pearl Buck had rented one for a number of summers, and our family used it over a two-year period for a two-week vacation. The house was a bit rough around the edges. There was one very large room with lots of chairs, many couches that doubled as beds, and a large dining room table. A small kitchen and a small bedroom completed the floor plan. Most of the modern conveniences were showing their age, but it was a pleasant retreat and an exciting change of pace for the family. The island was isolated. No typical New Jersey resort boardwalk or other bright light activities were present. It was quiet and restful.

A number of memories return. One was the drift-wood Pearl Buck had collected during her walks on the beach and displayed through the beach house. Each piece was an animal mutation creatively labeled. The rabboon, with a hulking body structure and an easily identified rabbit-shaped head, and the armadilladeer, as could be expected, a rounded, armored-appearing body with an antlered head, are two that come to mind. The children loved to play in the sand, and we older ones were frequently on the bayside crabbing and swimming in the warm water. The ocean side, without lifeguards and with a quick drop into deep water, was judged too dangerous. I remember an occasional, unwise plunge into the sea, but generally we would travel the short distance up the island to Seaside Heights for any ocean swimming that took place. Another memory that clearly marks this time period and illustrates the family interest in the sports world occurred on the boardwalk in Seaside Heights. There many of us were huddled around a portable radio listening to the 1950 All-Star baseball game. When Red Schoendienst, of my then-beloved St. Louis Cardinals, won the game with a home run for our favorite National League, the cheer we emitted drew a few stares. What was this crazy group doing jumping and shouting? Just our normal reaction to the sporting world, I guess. Just your "average" family on a seashore vacation enjoying themselves spontaneously.

More popular and certainly more memorable were the wonderful vacations spent in Vermont. Through the late 1950s and well into the 1960s, all looked forward with great anticipation to the annual trip. There in a comfortable cabin called Forest Haunt, the family spent two weeks each summer in a wooded setting that brought everyone close to nature. A beaver dam, maple syrup trees, isolation, porcupines, and outdoor cooking were just some of the atypical things that made the Vermont time so special.

Forest Haunt was one of the cabins that Pearl Buck had built on 2,000 acres of Vermont woodland she had purchased in the late 1940s. The land was situated at the foot of Mount Stratton. The first cabin, Mountain Haunt, was built as an escape site for Pearl Buck during the worst periods of her hay fever attacks. Eventually, two other cabins were built to provide housing for friends and visitors, and, of course, her Welcome House family members were some of the regularly invited guests. We older children were not part of the annual trek to New England after we began our summer jobs at Fischer and Porter. Only after I married and had my own children did we join the family for the summer retreat. Other friends, in particular the Bud Hollenbachs of Perkasie with their two sons, Jeff and Mark, became part of the annual stay in the mountains, and it was always a joyous gathering.

The reports of the Welcome House vacation are many—swimming at a nearby lake; going into Rutlege for an occasional bowling excursion; playing whiffle ball outside the cabin; taking long hikes through the woods; enjoying games inside the cabin, often around a blazing fireplace started to thwart off the cool Vermont nights. It was a relaxing setting and it had a major effect on family nurturing, I'm sure. The children all remember these times with great fondness. Though it is impossible to return to those times, they will never be lost. Through these experiences the children learned a great deal. Again, it was life away from the rural mores of Bucks County.

The printed media did not neglect Welcome House. Throughout the fifties, magazine editors felt the reading public would enjoy the Welcome House story. For example, *Life* magazine ran a feature on Welcome House in July of 1956. The article produced a great deal of publicity. The magazine, with its international circulation, gave Welcome House world-wide recognition. It also created a unique, personal anecdote, that prompts the cliché, "what a small world." By this time, I had begun college and had given college sweatshirts to my brothers and sisters. The children were wearing the Albright sweatshirts for the *Life* photographers, and the pictures reached my future in-laws in Belgium. It created quite a stir when the Albright name, previously unknown to them, was so prominently displayed in a major magazine. The *Reader's Digest, Ladies Home Journal*, and *Collier's* also included special articles on the Welcome House experience.

Perhaps, most appropriately, Welcome House received feature-story coverage in *Friends*, the organizational magazine of the Chevrolet division of General Motors. Chevrolet committed itself to family values during this decade. The middle class family was rapidly increasing (1.1 million new middle class families annually). *Fortune* magazine claimed the growth would produce "an economy of abundance" with optimistic philoprogenitive, high-spending, debt-happy, bargain-conscious, upgrading American consumers." Chevy was out to win the middle class consumers with its TV ads.

Kensinger Jones, a newly hired advertising director, used the television media to accomplish this. His ads were mini-stories and their emphasis was always family life. In one example, a young high school graduate was on his way to the prom. Smartly attired in his white dinner jacket, he waves his family good-bye and rushes to his jalopy. But his eye catches another car parked in front of the house. It's a brand new Chevy convertible. He turns back to the family on the front porch. Dad and sis smile at their secret. Dad reaches in his pocket for a set of keys. He flips them to his son, who races to the convertible and drives away, smiling, to pick up his "best girl." This is a great kid, a great family, a great car. The announcer closes the deal with, "What a gal! What a night! What a car! The New Chevrolet!" The advertising manager of Chevy broke into tears when he saw the ad.

Though apparently not television-worthy, Welcome House became a part of the Chevrolet promotion of family values. In *Family Magazine*, October 1953, the lead story was titled, "Welcome House is a Welcome Home." A brief comment on Welcome House and a half dozen pictures on the family gave national coverage to Pearl Buck's dream. It was welcome publicity, and it made all of us feel very proud. But, unlike Pat Boone, Chevy's big-name TV salesman, who annually received a station wagon and a Corvette, pride and publicity were all we received.

The two-page article says, through a few words and pictures, what I'm saying in this story. Welcome House was truly a welcome home. The media was yet another contact point between Welcome House and the world at large.

So, in hindsight, the Welcome House children were really not isolated. Though tied to the hearth to a greater extent than most of the kids in our community, they really had a lifestyle that was more cosmopolitan than anyone could imagine, considering our rural location. Their lives that began with such bleak prospects had become rich, full, and meaningful. Not only were my brothers' and sisters' lives so drastically changed and improved, but by their example, they were paving the way for thousands to follow. Now it is time to see how these children met life in church, school, and community.

— *Chapter 7* —

THE CHURCH AND
WELCOME HOUSE

The success of Welcome House may seem puzzling since the home originated in an age when many Americans were suspicious of any people with identifiable differences. A well-documented survey of popular attitudes collected in 1954 reveals the depth of the paranoia and ignorances of the times. Using data gathered by the Gallop Poll and the National Opinion Research Center, Samuel Stauffer reported that a majority of Americans had a fear and loathing of communism. Yet, at the same time, few could explain why. "He had a map of Asia on his wall." "He was always talking about world peace." "He handed out literature on the United Nations." "I don't know how, but I can tell one when I see him."

And, after the communist revolution in China in 1949, it was very easy to make these same, irrational comments about the Chinese. After all, they were communists, and our past racism toward Asian people made it very easy to interchange communist and Chinese. "They're all like that." With such sentiments in the air, any logical person would assume that a house full of Asian-Americans in the middle of rural Pennsylvania would certainly draw much suspicion and possible fanatical reaction in these early years of the 1950s, the era of the Joe McCarthy witch hunt. But it wasn't happening. Why?

Our parents were obviously quite good at their role. But Welcome House was not an island. The family had to circulate and eventually function in the outside world as well. Where would this take place, and what would be the reaction?

In these early years, a regular point of contact with the outside world was through our church. Every Sunday morning, all of us made our way to Souderton, a town about eight miles west of Blooming Glen, for services at the Zion Mennonite Church. There, in the "Welcome House" pew, our family worshipped with a congregation of caring and loving members. Friendship, love, concern, support—all of these were extended to the new children. It is unfortunately true that many American churches have been cited for hypocrisy in thought and practice. Many un-Christian values have been unleashed. Greed, racism, and violence have been condoned, or at least tacitly accepted, by too many established churches, and have caused cynics to raise serious questions about existing religion. But, it is my view that Zion Mennonite escapes the cynics' charge. On the issue of Welcome House, the people were good; their actions were generous; their support and love were unfailing. It began with our pastor, Ellis Graber, and carried throughout the rest of the congregation. Because the church role was so important to the well-being of Welcome House, I would like to share some of the details.

We were members of Zion for as long as I can remember. This attendance was just naturally continued with our new family. Dad was a long-time leader at Zion. At various times, he held all the important lay positions in the church—trustee, deacon, Sunday School teacher, Sunday School superintendent. He had the respect of all and was, as they say, "a pillar of the church."

Though history is filled with examples of "uncharitable Christians"—spreading Christianity through military conquest or forcing Jews into ghettos—the congregation at Zion was the product of a different historical tradition. The love and warmth extended to the growing family was a natural continuation of the Mennonites' long history of social concern. These seeds were planted in the century of religious protest and reformation of the 1500s. Resistance to state-imposed demands of war, taxes, or religion resulted in new theological ideals and eventual martyrdom for many followers. Menno Simons (source of the Mennonite name), Conrad Grebel, and others were leaders and martyrs who called attention to the movement and attracted many loyal followers. The *Martyrs Mirror* is a book that recounts such religious heroes and their lives, and the book continues to be second only to the Bible in the home of many Mennonites.

Within the larger framework of what was called the Anabaptist movement, which emphasized adult baptism and pacifism, the Mennonite church became an outspoken deterrent to mainstream actions that were judged to be anti-Christian, or inhumane, toward society as a whole. For this reason, many Mennonite groups challenged more than theological considerations and turned as well to many social issues. In recent times, supporting civil rights or contesting defense spending have become national causes for a body of concerned church goers who regularly venture into the world for social service.

Our church, Zion Mennonite of Souderton, Pennsylvania, is affiliated with the General Conference Mennonites. Members of this conference are sometimes referred to as "New Mennonites." Although adult baptism and pacifism continue to be central tenets to the religion, the conference, in contrast to other Anabaptist groups, places less emphasis on the need to follow anti-worldly personal values. As a consequence, the plain dress of "Old Mennonites" gives way to modern and changing clothing style; there is no rejection of new technology; more of the conference members have abandoned the rural lifestyle and are part of the complex, modern life without easily visible signs of their Mennonite origins. Nevertheless, New Mennonite association with the world at large may be responsible for the General Conference maintaining a high profile in struggling for social relief and social justice in a troubled society. Church concerns range from volunteer service for disaster relief to political commitment on war and civil rights.

The Mennonite Central Committee is an excellent example of this commitment. Mennonite volunteers have offered their services throughout the country for disaster relief. As an example, Wilkes-Barre, Pennsylvania, residents were especially appreciative of the Central Committee's effort in the aftermath of the floods from Hurricane Agnes in 1972. In more recent times, Mennonites hurried to Charleston, South Carolina, where Hurricane Hugo struck and destroyed so much of the old city. Likewise, church members often give weekend or vacation time to travel to some troubled spot to share carpentry or other talents, helping to relieve the tragedy of fire, flood, or poverty.

In addition, Zion was part of the mass demonstration in Washington, D.C., in 1963. Bus loads from Zion joined with Martin Luther King, Jr. and his followers as he shared his dream of a united America, "When little black children can join hands with little white children and walk through the fields of Georgia."

Thus, the traditional values and practices of the Mennonite Church cannot be overlooked as one searches for an explanation for the Welcome House success. In addition to the committed philosophy of Mennonites that would undoubtedly support a movement for social justice, such as Welcome House, members of Zion Mennonite took the Welcome House children into their hearts. Certainly Pastor Graber, as a close friend of the family, played a most significant role. Joining with other past ministers and leaders at the recent commemoration of Zion's 100th Anniversary, he included in his highlights of his years at Zion, his memory of the Welcome House pew, "second on the right, a row of happy faces, scrubbed and neat, singing and praying. Any hint of misbehavior was ended with a quick glance from the father or mother." Pastor Graber understood the complexities of the new age that was unfolding, and recognized the place and importance of Welcome House within this emerging racial pattern. I cherish his wisdom, his courage, and his love. He was one for the ages, and he certainly deserves credit as a significant participant in the Welcome House story.

Individual church members have numerous memories and reflections on these years. The Souders, Elvin and

Pattie, were my parents' closest friends. They remember these early times and, as mentioned earlier, were consulted by my parents when the Welcome House proposal was initially entertained. The Souders, as would be expected, have very fond memories and tell of the many conversations with Poppy and Ollie about the children. They have no knowledge of any Zion resistance to these children of different backgrounds, and they would have been shocked and offended if any had existed. For them, and apparently for Zion members as a whole, these were Yoder children. Other members have similar tales.

My brothers and sisters became an active part of the church body. Sunday School found them dispersed throughout different classes by age. Summer Bible School and occasional weeks at Men-O-Lan summer retreat put all of the younger children in touch with the rest of the children of Zion. Friendships of those years continue today.

Frank, Lillian, and I also had active roles in the church. Each Sunday evening, Rev. Graber met with the high-school-age church members. This youth fellowship was a religious and social experience that was very influential in developing our values and provided a major means of social contact and community entertainment for the older Welcome House children. The youths of Zion also participated in many group projects for relief. Paper drives, church and grounds clean-ups, or spring preparations for summer camps at Men-O-Lan are some examples of church service that expressed the Mennonite sense of community involvement.

Youth choir was a weekly activity with practice every Wednesday night, and regular participation in the Sunday morning service. Mrs. Graber was the choir director, and our church involvement contributed to a natural bridge between church, school, and community. In addition to our own church participation, our choir frequently sang at other churches.

Also, community and school contact is evidenced by the participation of many of our school and community friends in the choir. Four of the starters and the sixth man of our championship high school basketball team were choir members. The Grabers and many church members were frequent fans at our games. A good-spirited connection between church and school resulted. This was small-town life, and in a very natural and uncontroversial way, Welcome House children became part of the larger community. The pattern, begun in those early years, lasted throughout the maturing years of all my brothers and sisters. In this way, the church served as an entry into the community for the Welcome House children and a support system that responded in a multitude of ways. There can be no doubt that the Church and its members were vital to the well-being and success of Welcome House.

— Chapter 8 —

Welcome House
and the Schools

In the early 1950s, a national crisis in education was addressed by the Supreme Court of the United States. Arguing for integration of the public school system, Thurgood Marshall and the NAACP convinced the Court that a nation dedicated to equality could hardly make such a claim when its public schools were legally segregated and blatantly unequal. So in 1954, the Court declared in *Brown v. Board of Education of Topeka* that public schools must be integrated "with deliberate speed." A major institutional attack on discrimination was set in motion, and a new day in race relations seemed underway. We know now in the decade of the nineties that "deliberate speed" is hardly the speed of sound. Still, as the fifties began, there was emerging awareness of the social errors in race relations, particularly as applied to education. But the integration decision so necessary on the national level was not really applicable in the nearly all-white, rural Bucks County. Here the educational system was undergoing an integration of a different sort.

Welcome House was feeling the pains of an educational turmoil. Very different, and undoubtedly of far lesser magnitude, the crisis was nevertheless emotional and potentially disruptive. Welcome House children were proceeding through the various stages of youth and development. We older children were progressing through high school. Ray and Bobby were making their way through the elementary system, and the younger batch were going from happy, bottle-fed babies to frequently boisterous preschoolers. And so the day approached when these young ones would also have to venture into the world of education. This was certainly to be a new test. There was some natural apprehension in the hearts of my parents as this new chapter was about to begin. True, the older children were doing well in school, and had paved the way for this entry into the unknown, but for the little ones, it just seemed different. These were children who only knew the Welcome House family. Certainly, they were not isolated hot-house plants. They had regular community contact through church and community activities. David even had a preschool nursery class at the Doylestown Episcopalian Church, arranged by the Welcome House board, and family support was always available to ward off anything that seemed disruptive or threatening. In addition, each seemed to be self-confident and well-adjusted, so why the apprehension? Could some outrageous experience destroy all that had been so carefully nurtured?—a careless teacher? some thoughtless classmates? some prejudiced parents?

As stated, the older children were doing well in school; each had found a successful niche, with interests and friends, and had made the adjustment to the new family and school with relative ease. My father's presence at the high school, the involvement in athletics, my role as a contact to the system and classmates, and the strong personality and maturity of each of the older children made the entry into school rather smooth and uneventful. The path had been cleared, and now the younger ones had to find their own way through the system.

David again was the pathfinder. He was the first to enter this strange new world in the fall of 1952, and Mother reported the trauma of the first day when David, with his still bowed legs, reluctantly struggled off to meet the school bus. In this first year of his education, David was attending Hunsberger's School, a one-room school house about three miles from home. Hilltown Township was still using the many one-roomed schools that had been built in the early twentieth century. In fact, one of these, Leidy's

School, was the exact building where Dad had begun his career back in 1925.

Then, he was an eager nineteen-year-old, fresh from his two-year training from Millersville Normal School. When Dad began to teach, he had grades one through eight and taught all subjects. Each grade needed to have five major subjects taught each day (arithmetic, English, social studies, science, and reading) plus special periods of art and music mixed in. Can you imagine a school day divided into seven periods, with one teacher responsible for all the planning and enactment, and not for one grade, but for eight!? There were no free periods—no coffee breaks—no support staff. In addition to the teaching assignment, the single faculty member was responsible for all clerical reports and details, cleaning the school, building the winter fire, and bandaging the recess injuries. The only relief was the frequent use of the children for chores and details, and organized use of upperclassmen to aid the smaller kids in their lesson. This served both to occupy the older kids and increase the educational accomplishment of the younger ones. By modern educational standards, it seems a travesty. Today's magnificent school facilities, highly trained faculty, individual and specialized instruction, computer supports, innovative methods, etc., expose the old Hilltown system as hopelessly ineffective. Yet, with its obvious weaknesses, it must be recognized that the system did create a setting that promoted shared concern for fellow students and their success.

In a brief aside, I might add that my own interest in teaching began with the success felt in helping another student with his spelling list. During an oral spelling bee, my friend successfully spelled "education," a word I had reviewed with him. His pride, the astonished reaction of the class, since it seemed beyond his abilities, and the teacher's spoken praise to both of us—him for his accomplishment and me for my teaching—produced an exhilaration I have rarely felt since. In this environment, education goals were communal, and the method resulted in a school "esprit de corps"—a real concern for others and a true social conscience. Rewards were still granted to individuals through grades and teacher acclamation, but they were not attained by climbing over the backs of your peers. This spirit was obviously learned and carried into the community at large, and in my opinion was primary in forming the values of people in community, the kind who could accept a variant social arrangement such as Welcome House. Loving concern had become part of the people's nature.

Back to the school system. Through the years, changes were introduced into the one-roomed system. In particular, having eight grades in one room was discontinued. Four grades per room became the norm with grades one to four and five to eight grouped together. Eventually, upper grades were divided into schools for grades five and six, and one for grades seven and eight. Such a division made the school day less complex and confusing, but still provided ample opportunity for peer support and group development. These changes, introduced into the school system throughout the forties, were the basis for the education of myself and the older Welcome House children. This, too, was what David entered into at Hunsberger's School, still the one-roomed school with grades one through four. David's memory of first grade is limited, but he does recall some of the older children reviewing his spelling words and helping him with other school work through the system earlier described. David's days in this one-roomed system were to be short lived, however, for a new, fully equipped elementary school was to open in 1953.

This brand new school, teaching kindergarten through grade six, would become the site for the education of all the younger Welcome House children. In the new school's first year, David was entering second grade, and the second of the younger batch, Leon, would be a first grader. Sumi would follow the next year, and finally the "babies," Paul and Jack, in 1955. Thus, a veritable army of Yoders would invade the new facility, now called the Margaret Seylar Elementary School. The education was a totally new direction for the township. A central location in a rural setting with ample playground space, one grade per classroom, special teachers with special rooms for music and art, a multi-purpose room for lunch-time or indoor sports, a full-time support staff of janitors and secretaries, a building with all modern conveniences such as central heat and indoor plumbing (none of the original school buildings, including the high school, had indoor toilets, for example)—Hilltown Township education had entered the twentieth century. It should be noted that the high school would be closed after 1953, and all Hilltown students would be going to Perkasie as students in the new consolidation of school districts, Hilltown and Sellersville-Perkasie, into the Pennridge System. Within a year, a multi-million-dollar Pennridge High School would be completed for grades ten through twelve. Two junior high schools for grades seven through nine would also be established. Almost overnight, it seems, the educational system had been transformed. I would miss it completely, graduating with the last class from Hilltown High in 1953. Frank and Lillian would have a short time in the new system (one and two years respectively), but for all other children, the new elementary school and the large, new junior high and high school was to be their educational home. It was a sharp contrast to the old ways, but it offered the best in modern pedagogy.

A very important bridge between the old and new school systems, and Welcome House and the schools, was Mrs. Olive Solliday. Mrs. Solliday was my elementary school teacher, first through fourth grade, and she has many interesting memories about the early years in Blooming Glen, as well as the changing school system. By coincidence, she is part of the Welcome House story in various ways. She was a co-teacher with my father in the Blooming Glen Grammar School during the 1940s, after his years at Leidy's School and before his promotion to the high school. In the grammar school, Mrs. Solliday taught grades one through four in the first-floor room. And, in the only two-room elementary school in the system, my father taught grades five to eight on the second floor. Their teaching cooperation produced a friendship that lasted through our Welcome House years, and she and her husband John are examples of the supportive friends that allowed Welcome House to prosper.

Mrs. Solliday was also a key figure in the education of the small Welcome House children. Entering the new elementary system as a first grade teacher, Mrs. Solliday would be the teacher of two of the children, but she knew all of them, and was able to recall the school scene very well. For her, and apparently for all the staff and children, the Welcome House kids were like all the rest. They were good students; they did their homework (Dad made sure of that); they were well-dressed and neat (Mother's contribution); they were active at recess (a natural outgrowth of the Welcome House life); they were, in sum, good, normal kids going through typical school in a typical way. Racial problems, as reported from any who recall those days, were non-existent. This, of course, strikes me as a remarkable commentary considering the times, but is continuing testimony to the tolerance and fair ideals of the community and schools.

John Grasse was the Superintendent of the Hilltown Township Schools during those years. He remembers the conversation with Pearl Buck, when he recommended my Dad as tutor for her children. He also remembers telling my parents that the Welcome House idea was a good one. He dedicated his personal support to the project, and was quite sure that the school district would create no problem for the new children. He was one of the many local people who showed the necessary compassion to make Welcome House work. Looking back on these years, he was right about the openness of the schools, and of course, he was right to give the leadership that he did.

Time passed, and the children continued to make their way through the elementary grades. Now another emotional milestone was about to occur. They had to go from the local elementary systems into the Junior and

Senior High School mentioned earlier. The trauma that threatened, as one-room schools became the modern Margaret Seylar complex, paled before this next leap, for it must be remembered that the elementary school was still small and personalized, the students came from the same geographic area, and the school was physically situated across the fields from Welcome House, only two miles away. Now instead of Hilltown High School, with its 200 students being the culminating public school experience, the children had to join the large numbers that came from the far-reaches of the Pennridge District. Eight different communities fed the upper level grades. The comfortable, secure confines of the local district no longer surrounded the children. Here, they were cast into a whole new educational environment. What would their experience be? Was the anxiety felt a home a mistake?

A brief reply to the questions raised is simple, "there was no reason for alarm." The entry was smooth and uneventful. My brothers and sisters remember it in this way; the teachers of that era remember it in this way; Dr. William Keim, retired Superintendent of the Pennridge School System, remembers it in this way. In fact, the ideas of Dr. Keim serve as a general explanation of the children's new advance through the schools. Many of his words were repeated by others as they reflected on these years. In terms of the total family's attendance and graduation, they range from 1954, Franks's graduation, to 1969, Paul's graduation. The years when the younger children came to Pennridge Junior and Senior would be 1959-1969.

A continuing thought that ran through the conversations with the administration and faculty of those times was the influence of Poppy Yoder. The respect that he received from so many, converted into acceptance for whatever he said or did. Thus, the Welcome House experience carried no controversy, because it was part of Poppy Yoder's life. The same pattern of success in the Hilltown setting was repeated in the larger, all-encompassing Pennridge District. This was certainly true among the administration and faculty, and seems to have filtered down through the student body as well.

The Pennridge environment that produced an acceptance of the Welcome House children can be described in many ways. Though geographically and numerically larger, the district replicated many of the same positive attitudes present in the earlier school experiences. In a way, it was more of the same—tolerance, good spirit, love— generated at every level of the school community.

Credit must also be given to the Welcome House children. Infused with confidence inspired by our parents, my brothers and sisters became very successful members of the Pennridge system. On the one hand, each was active in the normal ways of high school students of that time. School activities included dances, clubs, dating, special friends for study-sessions, or just hanging out—these are the kinds of things all the kids became involved in. But the acceptance went beyond being an average student doing what most everyone else did. In a representative way, it is easy to illustrate the student leadership and involvement that made the Welcome House children more than average. Everyone of the children was at some time elected to the Student Council. David was President of the Council his senior year. Leon was a class president. Sumi was captain of the cheerleaders. Also, all were part of special student activities that brought them a kind of student acceptance through interaction and exchange. Prom committees, club leadership, or summer picnics at Welcome House are examples.

Truly, the activity that probably brought the greatest attention to the Yoder clan was the sports scene. True to the influence of our dad, all the young men became highly visible varsity athletes. In an age when women's sports were still struggling for parity, both Charlotte, before Pennridge, and Lillian, afterwards, were eager and successful participants. However, due to the unfortunate sex discrimination of the time, less was made of their success! Sumi made her way into the athletic world through cheerleading, becoming captain her senior year. All the brothers' success was remarkable.

Beginning with Frank in the fall of 1953, Pennridge football was treated to a bevy of Yoder half-backs, that continued through Ray, Bobby, Dave, and Leon. Each brought varsity letters to the Yoder honor roll, and all-league honors of Dave to the trophy case. Pennridge football in those days was extremely successful and much local fame was extended to all the participants. The local *News-Herald* was generous in printing the Yoder contribution to the Pennridge success, and at that time almost everybody loved a football hero, so the impact on the Welcome House image was certainly positive. Scott and Jack were also football players, Scott on the championship team of 1964, and Jack on a successful squad in 1967 and '68. Also, Paul was a very successful varsity wrestler; Frank, Ray, Bobby, Dave, Leon, and Jack were all varsity basketball players; David was a Pennridge record holder for the 220-yard dash (lasting over twenty years), and Leon and Bobby were sprinters on the track team. The list is an impressive one, I think, and the success certainly had to shower the Yoders with adulation and school popularity, but all of the children had been taught humility, and none was capable of truly misusing the kind of local celebrity status they achieved through sports. Dr. Keim and Bud Hollenbach, a coach and close friend of the family, echo this conclusion.

In this way, the Pennridge School can be seen as the large, consolidated institution that, nevertheless, had enough good-spirited members to make the education of these different children very normal in practice and outcome. That spirit may be best expressed by a school program that welcomed foreign exchange students with great enthusiasm. Dr. Keim told me that, for a period in the mid-sixties, Pennridge had proportionately the largest number of exchange students of any school district in this country. School and community cooperated to bring the foreign exchange students, to find housing, and to make the new students feel welcome. The spirit that provided this envi-

ronment was the type of good will that made the Welcome
House children a natural component of the student body.

Thousands of students were part of these years of
my brothers' and sisters' education, so it would be totally
naive to claim an absolute absence of any feelings of
intolerance or resentment. But, the inability to uncover
such sentiments through interviewing friends, teachers, and
the Yoders themselves, make it clear to me that good-
hearted tolerance was the rule, not the exception. The school
district and the many who were associated with the
children should take pride in their role. There was an
underlying sense of goodness. All the Yoders applaud
those good people as we look back with fondness on the
good times.

CHAPTER 9

THE COMMUNITY

Supporters of the glories of rural life are many, and their message comes in various forms. In an old melody, Dinah Shore sang about "the dear hearts and gentle people" that lived and loved in her hometown. Such nostalgia capturing the hearts and minds of people as they remember their origins is understandable, considering the pressures of a troubled contemporary world and the inexorable rush of time. Those whose roots are rural are further abetted in this yearning for the past by the plethora of images that have long described the countryside as that which is gloriously American.

A few sweeping reminders serve this conclusion. No less a figure than Thomas Jefferson extolled the virtues of the agrarian yeoman, and inveighed against the horrors of the sweatshops of industry. He felt America should be built on the benefits and the production of the rural community, not on the excesses of urban disorder. And images flash through our history—log cabin presidents, the wonders of nature, the frontier experience, kindly cooperation, later, the squalor of the early cities, the excesses of the industrial revolution, and later still, the growth of urban crime, relentless spread of urban physical decay, the pervasiveness of drug abuse. Is it any wonder that the image of the pristine life of the gentle glens, the fruited plains, or the majestic mountains has dream quality?

Some historians have added to this generalization. Lewis Atherton studied towns of the mid-west as they grew from 1865 to 1950. Separated from the urban centers, each town developed a life of its own. The townspeople had much pride in their way of life, and the virtues of their lifestyle was trumpeted throughout the Middle Border (the geographic area of his study). The message came from many quarters. *The Reader* of William Holmes McGuffey was a prime example. One hundred million copies were sold to Americans between 1850 and 1900. Used as the tool to teach reading to all young children, *The Reader* had an influence that was inestimatable. And it had a message—America was a classless society; opportunity was available to all who would seize it; God was in charge, and He had a plan; and also, rural life was superior to city life. Other positive endorsements for village life came from church sermons, chatauquas, newspapers, social events, and even high school commencement addresses. It was an overwhelming onslaught, and apparently, many people believed it. Henry Nash Smith in *Virgin Land* also offers a formidable array of historic voices who have affirmed the august place of agriculture and rural ways in American life. He quotes Benjamin Franklin. "The Great Business of the Continent is Agriculture. For one Artisan, or Merchant, I suppose we have at least 100 Farmers, by far the greatest past cultivators of their own fertile lands." St. John de-Crevecoeur, Thomas Jefferson, Abraham Lincoln, Walt Whitman, and Frederick Jackson Turner are others that Smith cites as supporters of rural virtue. Though selective, the message is ever present. Americans were promoting the efficacy of rural life, and considering the stature of speakers, their words had to be heard.

Not everyone accepts the glorification of the rural past. There is a flip side to the glowing assessment. Historians point out examples of rural life lacking harmony and social adjustment. Whether it be seventeenth-century witch hunts, eighteenth-century whiskey rebellions, nineteenth- and twentieth-century agrarian unrest, American history is filled with economic and social disharmony. Robert Dykstra discovered difficult times in the cattle towns of the west, where social discord and town-country conflict resulted in irrational political and social actions. Charles Beard wrote over fifty books about economic divisions and class struggles in America. In his interpretation, American progress came about, but only after the down-trodden rose up in protest. And some of the most vocal protests originated among rural people—Greenbackers, Grangers, Populists. This was not a scenario of happy, contented people, basking in the wonders of their existence.

Others may seem even less kind. In literature, mid-western towns were indicted in Edgar Lee McMaster's *Spoon River Anthology*. Sinclair Lewis shows Gopher Prairie, the town in his novel, *Main Street*, to be bigoted and parochial. There his heroine, Carol Kennicott, is trapped in a smug, inward-turning environment, that congratulated itself for its material success, and had no tolerance for differences, particularly ethnic or racial ones. Gopher Prairie was stifling and degenerative, and hardly the place you would want to raise a family.

As I ponder these many assessments of rural life, it seems clear that many of the values assigned to rural life, as per the McGuffey *Reader*, et al, are hardly the reality of the American past. The glories of the small town with its generous people and gentle lifestyle have been properly questioned and frequently found wanting. Yet the rhetoric has served to keep the possibility of the American dream alive for the multitudes. And so the dream continues, believed but not regularly substantiated.

My own estimates are generally optimistic. While I recognize the distorted and often exaggerated estimate of a glorious American past, I still believe there is an underlying goodness that flows through American life and has the potential to erupt at any time. People have charged me with a Panglossian view of the world and an overactive, nostalgic memory of the rural past, but I feel justified in questioning that charge. In particular, this evaluation is based on personal observation of the communities that were involved with the successful development of the Welcome House family. These particular communities are respectively—Blooming Glen, Dublin, and Doylestown. And each played a very significant role in this story.

Undoubtedly, the bigots of Gopher Prairie would not have been very receptive to the Welcome House model. Similarly many real towns of the American past, while claiming their humane qualities, would have been hard pressed to tolerate significant racial or ethnic differences. Such contrast to the communities that gave strength and sustenance to Welcome House is revealing. For it is my contention that here the myth of the past came to life. Maybe even McGuffey would be proud. Certainly, this was not Gopher Prairie.

Blooming Glen was the principal center of our activity since our original family came from there. Dublin, geographically closer to Welcome House, served as our economic source—food, garage, and restaurant. Doylestown, the county seat, added local prestige and financial support through many influential citizens and fundraising activities. All were important and deserve great credit for the Welcome House story. Without the love and support from each, the results of the social experiment would have been quite different, I'm sure.

Beginning with Blooming Glen, it is possible that nostalgic reverence may distort the Blooming Glen scene a bit. In my memory, the historic town was brimming over with excessive goodness, open charity, and freely-shared kindness. Does the evidence support such a charitable description? If it does, it becomes more understandable why Welcome House had such success in this small rural countryside. It is true Blooming Glen was the major focus of the Welcome House life. Here were our roots, our friends, and our schools. We knew virtually every household in the small village, and we were constantly interacting with those who lived there. Certainly Blooming Glen exemplified so many of those wonderful ways of rural life that have been glorified through the ages. Though they may be mythical elsewhere, I believe they were real in Blooming Glen.

How does one best uncover the essential goodness of a community? For it follows that such goodness, once demonstrated, would naturally contribute to the social experiment within its midst. For me, there are two rather distinct tracks that should be identified. One is to examine and report on some of the specific institutional configurations in the town, in particular the economic and educational ones. And second, is to relate some specific personal examples that do reveal the "dear hearts and gentle people that live (lived) in my hometown." (Now Dinah Shore would be proud.) The community of Blooming Glen with its people, its economics, and its general lifestyle was earlier introduced. Let me continue the narrative.

Perhaps it all began with the name. What could be more serene and peaceful than a blooming glen? Local tradition explains that the town was named in the early 1880s. Postal authorities requested an official name for the crossroad town locally called Moyer's Store. A flowering meadow nearby on the farm of Levi Moyer seemed a more appropriate local designation than the corner store of John Moyer (later to become Bishop's Store). And so the crossroad community with a store, a tavern, and a few houses came to be Blooming Glen. Slowly it grew through the early twentieth century as a community that joined with the surrounding farms and developed an ethos and identity of its own.

In effect, the town's economic institution served as the underpinning of a secure and well-functioning community by the 1940s. Most businesses operated without local competition—one barber, one shoemaker, one farm equipment store, etc. There were few complaints, and the business prosperity produced income that was dispersed throughout the community. In this way a successful butcher increased the economic well-being of others in the community, and his efforts were praised not questioned. This was a place that believed in the work ethic.

The butter and egg men seemed to be the best practitioners of that philosophy. This business was built upon a number of actions. In essence, the system provided an effective conduit for marketing much of the local produce through individually developed routes throughout the

Philadelphia suburbs. Each of the hucksters, as they were sometimes called (not perjoratively, however) had a walk-in panel truck, and his own particular way of filling it. Some prepared specialties such as pork products, chickens, or sausages. In most cases the wives were active participants and greatly aided in the preparations for marketing. All utilized the surrounding farms for vegetables in certain seasons—corn, tomatoes, and the like. And of course, the sales proceeds came back and provided a major boost for the local economy. It should be noted that here, too, the efforts were cooperative, not competitive, for the farm products were abundant and individual routes did not overlap.

Vital services completed a smoothly running, economic exchange. From medical care to dress making, the community was self sustaining and able to meet all basic needs. Cars were repaired by Earl Frankenfield; shoes were mended by Melvin Bishop; hair was cut by Ben Waldvogel; piano lessons were given by Alice Gulick; dressmaking and other special sewing assignments were completed by Ella Gross. All was done well and with a smile. In 1950, Dr. George Schaeffer became the new town doctor. Dr. Clarence Myers, who had served the community for decades, had retired. Fortunately, he had been around to stitch little ten-year-old Poppy Yoder's face when a sledding injury left him with a severe cut across his nose. Always he was here when the townspeople suffered all manner of illness, and he helped to heal and keep a community strong and obviously secure. He was important, but just one among many.

Those who worked at the U.S. Gauge in Sellersville, the pants factory in town, or similar occupations in nearby places also contributed to the success and stability of the little country village. In all cases a middle class standard of success was the rule. The system produced a happy contented population.

Another example of community cooperation was the grocery business. One might wonder about the economic consequences of two grocery stores in such a small community. The possibility of serious competition with perhaps subtle charges of false marketing practices or inferior products seemed a likely outcome. But such conflict never really happened. Trouble was most likely averted by the good spirit of the grocers, I suppose, and by the system of many of the townspeople. I can hear our neighbor, Katie Moyer, speaking now. "One week I go up to shop at Shaddinger's Store, the next week I go down to buy at Bishop's Store." (The Moyer's home was on the main street hill between the two stores, so up and down is a geographic reference.) It could also be pointed out that the son of one of the grocers, the son-in-law of the other, and the sons of the clerks of the competing grocery stores were all members of the local baseball and later, softball teams. They were friends and teammates, not economic competitors. The real concern was how to control the powerful sluggers of the Plumsteadville Stump Jumpers or the new, windmill pitcher of Butch Crouthamel's Dublin team. These were things to get emotional about.

The grocery stores were the scenes of much community social life. Each store had a front porch that was a favorite spot for summer time debates among the village youngsters. Also, the after-school gathering for soft drinks or other snacks was a regular experience. Debates were hardly the type that resulted in great social change. Repeated topics included: the best brand of soda (Coke was in last place because the bottles were too small), the best tractors (John Deere was in last place because it looked fragile with its thin body), the best bike (Roadmaster was in last place because my Roadmaster rusted and had a broken rear axle on three different occasions), the best President (F.D.R. did not play well in our Republican environment, and on this one we parroted our elders). By contrast, the consensus for best, although consistency was not our forte, would generally be Orange Nehi (Sorry, Radar, not grape, but the big bottles were influential), Farmall tractors (big and solid looking, and for me, one my dad drove working at the stone quarry), Schwinn (reputation, even in those days), Washington or Lincoln (pictures on school walls, songs, and celebration). It was innocent and emotional, but I never remember it escalating to any type of permanent estrangement.

Friday and Saturday night the Blooming Glen stores had a different group of customers. On those nights, the families from the nearby farms came into Blooming Glen, filling the town with good friends, shopping, and visiting. In hindsight, and compared to contemporary entertainment, this was rather unexciting and pedestrian. But it was a change from the daily routine, providing opportunities to catch up on any local gossip, have some "store-bought" refreshments, or visit with town friends. Since there was no movie theater, all entertainment was people oriented, and thus strengthened the friendly spirit so apparent in the community.

But the most important social happening that took place at the grocery store was the nightly gathering for the mail delivery. Shaddinger's was also the Blooming Glen Post Office and every night the scene would be the same. The townspeople would assemble to collect the daily mail, generally distributed by 6:30 p.m. At this time of day, Shaddinger's Store was the place to be. Inside the store, on the community bench, the men would exchange solutions for every conceivable social ill. Weather permitting, the teenagers would congregate on the front porch, teasing the opposite sex, or in their absence, talking about the opposite sex. We younger kids would be playing on the lawn and parking lot. In particular, we would be using the hitching rail as a type of early jungle gym, since it was no longer used for horses. The scene was a happy one, filled with friendship, good spirit, and joy.

Somehow, in this isolated environment, the world problems were analyzed and verbally solved. Most felt that all would be fine if only our local wisdom prevailed. My first knowledge about the dangers of atomic weaponry came from eavesdropping on one of these conversations. I discovered that the next atomic test would most likely set off an irreversible chain reaction of atomic explosions, only ending when the earth was destroyed. This and other discussions greatly tormented my young mind. Where did God come from? Are Hitler and Roosevelt hiding out together in Argentina? Do you get polio from swimming in infected water? After many sleepless nights worrying about the consequences of such dilemmas, I decided that I would only listen in on discussions about the greatest ball player of all time, or which tractor was the most effective— the Farmall or the John Deere. (My choices were Stan Musial and Farmall.)

In retrospect, it is now apparent that these gatherings were a major social outlet for the people. Not everyone came each night, but there was a representative of each family there almost every night. I should note here that, while Blooming Glen had an apparently tolerant strain that would accept the new racial approach of Welcome House, the traditions of male/female roles were more firmly entrenched. The women were not typically part of this scene. This was the time of day to clean up the kitchen after the evening meal. The men or children would retrieve the mail. The opportunity for social discourse, knowledge that people would be available for discussion, the chance to have ice cream or a coke, all made this a happening and it was friendly interchange. Debate was enthusiastic, but never really hostile.

Though the exclusion of women was an unfortunate tradition of the time period, the town, in general, was an open society with all participating and feeling accepted. In conclusion, the security that came from the economic system, resulted in a happy community of people that really liked each other. This economic cooperation just naturally spilled over into many other areas of community life and helped make the community the happy place it was.

Another focal point for community interaction was the school. This discussion, in some ways, overlaps with the earlier assessment of education and its impact on Welcome House. In reality, all the institutions that supported Welcome House had points of intersection, but Hilltown High School, geographically located in the center of Blooming Glen was a significant contributor to the Blooming Glen social activities, particularly as it existed before the Pennridge consolidation in 1953. Hilltown High School activities were really community activities.

To begin with, the high school offered numerous programs that were very important to the people. Drama presentations were a good example. Traditionally, the Community Hall was used for plays and special programs. After it became an agricultural center, the show moved to Souderton High School. The nights of the performances were not good ones for door-to-door sales in Blooming Glen. Everyone was in Souderton. Occasionally, a movie was shown in the high school. Folding doors were moved, and people crowded into the double room of the high school, sharing seats, sitting on the floor, or standing in the back. I remember seeing *Abe Lincoln in Illinois* in this fashion. It was an impressionable movie, not just for a little person, but for the town as a whole. Abe Lincoln was a Blooming Glen-kind of person.

Sometimes the community welcomed a special guest. A young Bayard Rustin came to Blooming Glen in 1949, I believe, before he became a well-known Civil Rights leader. He had been a guest speaker at our church, Zion Mennonite, and my dad invited him to Blooming Glen for a lecture as well. He spoke to a full audience in the new gym, and his remarks were not the every-day fare of local life. I recall he spoke about black life, and he also offered a philosophical description of the origins of life. The reaction to the speech was quite remarkable, in my opinion. Most of those in attendance had little contact with black Americans at that time and, I'm sure, rarely thought much about black life. Also, his biological descriptions of life's origin was totally at odds with the community's belief in the Garden of Eden. I can still see him contorting his body and throwing up his arms in a symbolic representation of life emerging from the mud and water of the earth. Undoubtedly, most of the people there believed the biblical account of the origins of life; yet their reaction was warm and friendly.

Comments in the following days, directed to my dad, made it clear that Blooming Glen was proud to be associated with the young black intellectual. What a commentary on Blooming Glen. While the Yahoos were booing Jackie Robinson and Larry Doby for stepping over baseball's color line, a little rural Pennsylvanian community was warmly entertaining a young, black activist. Perhaps "only in America" is the accurate appellation here. Or, is it "only in Blooming Glen"?

Another interesting community lecturer was Joseph Yoder, a writer and musician. He came during the same time period as Rustin, but no records are available to specifically date his visit. It seems he was a distant cousin of my dad, but they did not know each other before his arrival. He came to talk about his book, *Rosanna of the Amish*, and stayed at our house for a few days. Joseph led the community in an enthusiastic sing-along and then talked about his book, an unusual example of what today we think of as the need for cultural diversity. His story described a little Irish girl who was raised by Amish people and maintained her identity in a cultural setting totally unknown to her. The message of his book, his own open-mindedness, and our community's enthusiasm for him and his work is just one more vivid illustration of a tolerant people going about their business, but recognizing the rights and dignity of others.

The school also served as an important community function through the sports program. We had many fans, both from the student body and the community, who shared regularly in our successes and failures. One of the clearest examples of town/school cooperation and the community involvement with athletics was the building of our gymnasium.

Prior to 1945, the Community Hall had been an all-purpose center that could be converted into a small, but functional, basketball court. However, the decision to convert the hall into an agricultural center, earlier noted, eliminated its use as a gym. For three years, my father organized night trips to Perkasie, or later the National Farm School in Doylestown, for basketball practices. The makeshift arrangement provided some practice time, and the development of teams, both men and women, that played a limited number of organized games with other schools. And, of course, without a home gymnasium, all games were played on the opponents' home court.

In 1948, my father, weary of the struggles to find an open gym, decided we should build a facility of our own. School funds were unavailable, so other avenues had to be explored. A few neighbors, Len Iles and Ralph Moyer, were initially contacted for ideas. Together, they recruited other sports enthusiasts and a plan was formulated. Individual businesses would be solicited for $200 donations. The men would pool their talents; lumber would be secured at a cut rate; a somewhat temporary structure would be built, basically as a practice facility. The school board allowed the structure to be placed on an outdoor basketball court behind the high school.

With community volunteers, the work began, and before the first frost of 1948, a gym had arisen. Hardly a palace, it was still a local treasure. Simply a wooden frame covered with beaver board sides, a shingled roof, and a potbellied stove for heat, it nevertheless was a gym, and a crowning example of what can be achieved by spirited cooperation. It was a fine practice facility compared to what preceded it. The high school teams benefited greatly, although they continued to use rented gyms for games. Fortunately for me and my grammar school friends, special practice time was set aside for us as well. And it was the first step toward a permanent structure.

The next spring, the school superintendent, John Grasse, came to see my dad. The school board needed more space for classrooms. Someone got the idea of expanding the gym. The plan was to use the basic frame, put the building on permanent footings, replace the beaver board with wood and siding, and cover the asphalt floor with a smooth, painted surface. Grandstands and benches would provide about 300 seats. There would be a dressing room with showers. A large bank of windows would cover one side of the building. For the interior, there would be a movable divider, making two large classrooms for daytime, with a full-time gym for afternoons and evenings. Mr. Grasse talked to my father about this proposal because the school had not participated in the original building. However, I remember the eagerness with which my dad endorsed the plan. This was certainly a major improvement for the athletic program and a moment to savor. For my dad, it spelled progress.

The conversion of the gym took place during the summer of 1949. My freshman class was the first to use the new building. By contemporary standards, it was quite inadequate. As a gym, the court was too narrow; the floor too hard; the seating too cramped; and the shower room too small. Its classroom function was also less than perfect. The room divider was not soundproof; blackboard space was meager; the classroom environment was not educationally sound. But the complaints were nonexistent. This was a special place, and for four years, it was the scene of many joyous moments.

The completed gym was the result of the community's cooperative spirit. Sociology supports this conclusion. Evon Vogt and Thomas F. O'Dea described two communities that were going through similar educational and athletic needs about the same time the Blooming Glen effort took place. The communities, Rimrock and Homestead, were rural New Mexico farm villages. Both needed a gym. Rimrock, with a cohesive, well-organized, and cooperating community structure built around their religious unity, formulated a plan and successfully completed their project. Homestead, without common identity and cohesiveness, found their gym plan collapse with only half a building erected. The sociologists conclude that a unifying social pattern (in this case religion) was the primary reason for Rimrock's success, and lack of prior community structure was the reason for Homestead's failure. The successful completion of our gym paralleled the Rimrock experience and strengthens my contention that Blooming Glen was a place with generous qualities— whether it be building a new gym or supporting an unusual social experiment.

The gym was a godsend to our school and community. It rocked with excitement whenever our teams competed. Our school was very successful in all sports, but basketball became our favorite, thanks to the new building.

Frank, with his aforementioned muscular build, proved to be an excellent athlete. He was, from the beginning, a very visible presence in the school system, and a very positive one. His athletic success made him a local hero; significantly, he was a Welcome House child who became a source of community pride. The Perkasie weekly, *The News Herald*, carried all of our sports results, so even those who couldn't attend games knew about our team. Thus, Frank was Welcome House's first sports ambassador, and he served with distinction. In a sports-minded community, he played an invaluable role, proving how talented, yet typical, the Welcome House children could be.

One might question the legitimacy of securing public acceptance of Welcome House because of athletic success. In truth, this only aided the process. And because it was low key, I find little to criticize. It was innocent adulation and, as I said earlier, it continued as the younger children found athletic success after advancing into the Pennridge consolidation. Their role as local athletes endeared them to the community. Though the children were involved with the community in other ways as well, the sports connection, because of its popularity, certainly influenced the community's acceptance of Welcome House.

A brief digression provides some detail on the place sports had in our lives, and the impact that our gym had on me personally. A few years ago I took a group of Albright faculty to view the Christmas decorations at the Pearl Buck house, a regular feature of the homestead since it became a historic site in 1981. Motoring along in a fifteen-passenger van, the group and I spent most of the hour bantering back and forth—I glorifying my place of origin versus their charges of Hicksville and the like. Though Pearl Buck had great meaning for them, Blooming Glen apparently had none. Included in my comments glorifying the tradition of my community was the important function of our gym. Comparing it to Yankee Stadium as the House that Ruth Built, I tried, immodestly, to generate the feeling that this was the House that Yoder Built.

As we passed through Blooming Glen and entered the lane alongside our former high school, I prepared for the moment with a loud tooting of the van horn and an emotional, "And here it is!" Pure shock followed. The gym wasn't there. Unknown to me, the township had taken over the high school building and had added a large room that stretched out near the gym. The gym was then removed to make space for parking cars. The moment offered a scene of hilarious good fun, since I had built it up with such enthusiasm while local politics had seen fit to remove our historic treasure. My laughter was contrived; the tears in my eyes were real. True, it was probably analogous to the Model T Ford that served its purpose and faded as technology found new ways to produce speed and power. But the past dies hard. The site that served us all so well may be gone, but it lives forever in our cherished memories. It was a major reason for our community's *espirt de corps.*

Local sports had a unifying effect on our community in many ways. The sports scene was a frequent topic for the community bench discussions at both Shaddinger's and Bishop's stores. A base hit, sacrifice, base hit sequence that beat Springfield High School in the last inning of the 1952 championship game brought this reaction. "It looked like Connie Mack's A's in action." Though grossly exaggerated, it was great fun and the source of much community pride. An incredible basketball victory over arch rival Coopersburg, in the winter of 1953, was one of the most exciting and unusual athletic events I've ever been involved in. In the middle of the fourth quarter, we were thirty points ahead of the team that had beaten us earlier in the season. Unaccustomed to such luxury and still feeling insecure about the outcome, I remember questioning my dad's wisdom when he substituted for the first team.

"Sit down and relax," he said rather abruptly. "Even Jimmy Schaeffer can't bring Coopersburg back tonight." Jim Schaeffer was the Coopersburg star who went on to have a long career in professional sports as a catcher and coach for the St. Louis Cardinals. That victory was a bright and long-serving topic of conversation at the community benches.

The following Saturday morning session was a joyous one. Eager to bask in the local adulation, I remember dropping by the stores to hear the day-after reflections. I recall one comment about a behind-the-back pass that led to an easy, and somewhat spectacular, field goal. In truth, it was a pass that went astray that somehow found a teammate. That was the kind of night it was. I didn't admit to the luck of it then. Unfortunately, the truth of the act now becomes a matter of record. Maybe Jim Moyer, a close friend of the family and brother-in-law of one of my teammates, won't remember the conversation. At any rate, confession is good for the soul. And similar discussion continued until the day the stores closed.

Speaking to some of the old-time residents, I find my memories confirmed. One area that was rife with community spirit and good times was the summer sports scene. In the days before Little League, my dad came up with an idea to organize a local baseball league. It was a most unusual construction. Three teams were formed and rather strangely labeled the Donkeys, the Elephants, and the Tigers. Dad purchased inexpensive sweatshirts and solicited high school players to not only lead the teams, but also to play. So, here was a competitive league that included players who were juniors and seniors in high school, as well as youngsters that were twelve and thirteen years old. It strikes me that an unusually high sense of tolerance and brotherly love must be practiced for such a system to work.

The high school players were members of some very successful teams, and here they were enthusiastically mixing with the little kids. For me, personally, the words of Tiger player-coach Paul Buehrle was an early lesson in confidence building. To an intimidated sixth grader, he said, "You can play second base for us, and you'll do well." He probably was wrong, but it surely sounded good to me. I remember Marvin Landis, a high school student and catcher on our team, stopping by our front porch and discussing strategy on how we would beat Sam Stover's Donkeys that night. He made a little sixth grader feel pretty significant. Without a doubt, this was a special community.

The men's softball team also produced tremendous community spirit. This team replaced the previous Blooming Glen baseball team during the war years when many of the younger players were in the service. After the war, the softball team continued. I remember the softball games in the years before Welcome House. At that time, most of the games were played in Dublin, under the lights at Butch Crouthamel's field. Blooming Glen and Dublin were heated rivals then, and the games were always exciting. My dad was the Blooming Glen pitcher, and I remember how proud I felt when the Blooming Glen fans cheered his exploits. Nearly all the townspeople traveled to Dublin, because everyone wanted to defeat the feisty Butch Crouthamel and his "overrated" teams. And we usually did just that.

In 1946, the Blooming Glen Athletic Association decided to put lights on the Blooming Glen field. They would be superior to the Dublin field—six poles rather than four, more lights on each pole, and stronger light poles reaching at least ten feet higher in the air. Blooming Glen, the superior team, would now have the superior field as well. In addition to the lights, new bleachers, a new backstop, and a hot dog stand made our field the "best in Pennsylvania."

It wasn't, of course, but on game nights the town was filled with fans from all over. The streets were lined with parked cars, and the crowd filled the bleachers, often lining left and right field, three deep. It was a community experience in an age when life was simpler. Our interests were local. Technological competition (TV, easy transportation, etc.) was on its way, but not yet available for everyone. Thus, community activities were more important, more central to everyone's life. The result was a socially responsible, thriving community—the kind that would welcome Welcome House. Like so much of this story, it was a nice combination.

Maybe the words of a long-time resident say it best. Recent Xeroxed collection of memories from Blooming Glen included the following:

Thinking Back in Blooming Glen

One beautiful spring morning, a little girl was born right in the center of Blooming Glen, Pennsylvania. It was just a few short steps for the doctor to take to come to help in this big event as Dr. Meyers lived just across the street from my parents' home. As I grew older, I can remember my friend, Eleanor, would come and play on our back porch and walks. Sometimes the bigger girls and boys—like Bill and Edna—would talk to us over the fence.

When I was six years old my daddy purchased the farm north of town. This would be my first year to go to school and I would have to walk all by myself down to the inter-section and hope to meet someone there. Sometimes I would take the bypass—a path which I made through Levi Moyer's meadow and over Mabel Bishop's bridge—coming on Route 113 at the corner where the gas station now stands. For eight years I was privileged to do this, going to the best school in the township and having two of the best teachers around—Miss Yoder, later to become Mrs. Solliday, and Mr. Yoder. I often dreamed of what it would be like to ride a "Yellow School Bus." Some days Mr. Yoder would make us hot split pea soup and other days he would tell us to

*bring a cheese sandwich the next day and he would toast it
for us in a grill he held over the heater.*

*Saturday evening was our big night out as we would
go shopping or for groceries at Bishop's or Shaddinger's
store. Here I would probably meet Jean and Doris, as their
parents were shopping, too. I was always sort of
envious of Elizabeth and Paul Buehrle, as every Saturday
night at 9:00 p.m. their dad would come over to Bishop's
store with a big bowl and Elmer would dip it heaping full
of all flavors of ice cream. How yummy it looked!*

*Then, occasionally the Auxiliary would present a play
at the community hall. I loved going to these and also to
hear "Lizzie Hoa." Every fall, the auxiliary put on the
best chicken suppers, family style. The price is unbelievable, adults, $.75 and children, $.25. My parents always
mashed all the potatoes (by hand, with small potato
mashers). Ella Gross made the best filling—frying it in the
black cast-iron fry pans on the coal-oil stoves. Emma
Shaddinger was busy cutting all the pies the ladies made;
I can especially remember Lilly Bishop's meringue pies,
just perfect. (More evidence of the community cooperation
represented here. Emma was the wife of Henry Shaddinger,
the "uptown" grocer; Lilly was the wife of Garwood Bishop,
the "downtown" grocer.)*

*This town had so many pleasant memories for me, I
finally planted my husband here and raised my two daughters on a much more traveled Route 113, but it is still home
and our roots are planted firm in our church and schools.*

Also in the Xeroxed collection is the following statement from a schoolmate of mine and presently a neighbor
of my sister Charlotte. Betty Jane Detweiler Moyer writes,
"We have visited places from Alaska to Hawaii, but it is
always great to come back to Blooming Glen, of which I
have been a resident all my life."

And Mahlon Souder, a good friend of my father, and
a significant community voice throughout his life wrote
these words:

>*The Blooming Glen people have not changed. The friendliness of the people is still the same as ever. The late H. R. Shaddinger, as we were taking a drive out into the country, said, "It is not in us to do big things—how true. Things have not changed. The smile of a little child. The fragrance of the flowers. The song of the birds—they are still the same. . . . As we are writing these notes, it is a beautiful day in Blooming Glen and I have now lived 30,869 days. The Lord has been very good to me. As we grow older, we should take more time for meditation, for prayer, and reading God's Word. Someone has said a feeling heart and a responsive body know no retirement age. I agree. Yes, Blooming Glen is a beautiful place to live in."*

Do the above words prove the essential goodness and kindly tolerance as claimed? Should I also include the many times neighbor Amy Iles nursed me through cold and fever while Mother worked? The backyard cookouts at Erv Moyer's? The croquet games at Bob Moyer's? The late night trips to buy a milk shake or other treats with Ralph or Ethel Moyer and children? The shared vacations with numerous neighbors? (Lake Gilman, Lake Harmony, the New Jersey Coast) The unlocked doors?

History shows that this was a community whose religion, education, and shared values resulted in harmony and justice. It was a time to cherish, and there is no doubt in my mind that these were gentle, kindly people who rallied around a noble undertaking like Welcome House and helped it succeed. They proved it in so many ways.

Dublin was the second community to touch the lives of the Welcome House residents. But this was a different type of interaction. This was not a town where we knew every person and household. Rather, we were directed toward specific economic enterprises. For example: Earl Frankenfield, the Blooming Glen garage man, had died and Butch Crouthamel became my dad's garage man. It seemed a bit strange. In my young mind, Butch had been the leader of the Dublin softball opponents, and it didn't seem quite right to cozy up to our old enemy. That feeling soon passed. Butch was fine, and his mechanics were outstanding. Dublin Garage could take care of our cars. The past adversarial relationship with Butch and Dublin faded into oblivion.

Goldie's Diner was another Dublin base. In the years before Welcome House, our family had gone to Goldie's for evening meals on frequent occasions. My dad's busy schedule and my mother's regular job made dinner preparation difficult. So, we had been regular customers at Goldie's as long as I can remember. After Welcome House, the trips to Goldie's were less frequent. Still, Lyd and Goldie Meyers, the owners, were good friends and the family always felt welcome when the periodic spaghetti dinners, or other low-cost meals, became a special event for the Welcome House family. Dinner at Goldie's was exciting and provided another opportunity for bringing children into contact with the community. This was not Gimbel's dining room. Welcome House children were not viewed here as social aberrations. The size of the family was a greater attraction than the composition of the family.

We also bought our groceries in Dublin. This might seem unusual since our family had been so close to the Blooming Glen grocers. But there were reasons for this switch. Our ties to the Blooming Glen grocery business were lessened by the following. First, the Dublin grocers were Herbert Stauffer and Sons. The Stauffers were some of the early, involved supporters of Welcome House. Their friendship, through membership in our Zion Church and their constant concern for our family's needs, made them logical recipients of our business. Also, our house was only one mile from Dublin, compared to two miles from Blooming Glen, so Stauffers offered the convenience of proximity. Also, Henry Shaddinger had sold his store and, while the new owner, Warren Horricks, was a fine man, there was no life-long friendship here. Bishop's Store was harder to forsake, and I know my parents continued to patronize the store on occasion just because of the friendship and good feelings toward the Bishops.

But the most important reason for the switch to Stauffers was the influence of Pearl Buck and the Welcome House Board. Since Stauffer was Pearl Buck's grocer, and since she had placed special orders with them for a long time (for example, the whole grain brown bread mentioned earlier), it was natural that she would expect our family food shopping to be where special and, in her mind, necessary foods were available. In those early years, before Mother received a set monthly food allotment, the food was charged at Stauffers (with limits) and Welcome House paid the bill. In this way, Dublin and the Stauffer shopping trips became part of the regular routine of the family.

Dan Stauffer told me that just as his dad had talked with pride about the community opportunity to serve when Welcome House began, so he and his family continued in that feeling as Mother, Dad, and the children grew and patronized the Dublin store. He and his wife Florence were among the many persons who echoed the community good will toward Welcome House.

It is unfortunate that so many of the Dublin people who interacted with Welcome House during these formative years are no longer with us. Herb Stauffer, Butch Crouthamel, Goldie Meyers, and Sam Moyer are all gone. Another was Dad's sister, Katie Keeler. She lived in Dublin with her husband Oswin, and frequently helped Mother during the canning and freezing season. She also made the most delicious meat pies, and at least once a year the whole family would gather for meat pie and pickled cabbage—a meal that, once eaten, will never leave your memory. Her involvement with the family was quiet testimony to the kind of love that was generated by so many. Without such support, it is hard to imagine how Welcome House would have worked.

So, it is apparent that Dublin was crucial to the development of the Welcome House family. Each of the persons mentioned served in some way to further the growth and maturation of the family.

The last of the communities, Doylestown, was more distant, both geographically and emotionally. Yet, here again, many people were instrumental in the Welcome House growth. It is true that these people were not family friends when Welcome House began. Their connection with Welcome House came through Pearl Buck. It was her name and her persuasive message that attracted the Doylestown support for the humanitarian undertaking. Our paths would probably never have crossed without Welcome House. Still, great love and cooperation grew between all of us.

Judge Edward Beister, the son of the original board members, Edward and Muriel Beister, remembers the beginning of Welcome House quite clearly. Judge Beister and his wife have followed in the path of his parents in supporting the growth of the Welcome House movement. At a recent dedication of a new wing to the Welcome House Adoption Agency in Chalfont, Pennsylvania, he spoke with conviction about the role of the Yoders in breaking down the barriers that had once made Asian-Americans impossible to place. He recognized the sacrifice and praised the commitment of the Yoders as parents. In an interview after his public remarks, he repeated these feelings, and also commented on the Doylestown community and his evaluation of the community response to the Welcome House needs.

Support for the organization came in various forms. To begin with, many of the board members had Doylestown ties—if not specifically in the borough, then on the periphery. The Beisters, Burpees, and the Fischers of the original board were all part of the Doylestown community. The Hammersteins; the Micheners; the realtor, Herbert Barness; and the Busby Taylors were either from Doylestown or the surrounding countryside. In addition to the financial support, these people served as important local figures who, by their participation, made a positive statement for racial changes. Also, many gave of their time. Besides the actual board meetings, many visited the children or hosted the

Welcome House family for picnics or parties. Also Busby Taylor, in his retirement days, frequently came to Welcome House to perform handyman chores. Such service made Welcome House succeed.

Dr. Harriet Davis is another of the Doylestown people who played a significant role in the Welcome House story. Her service as the children's doctor was a source of great comfort for my parents. Always available, she provided professional security that lessened the pressure of the child-rearing responsibilities my parents felt. Her medical expertise and her kindly counsel were invaluable as the family grew and prospered.

In addition, Doylestown people committed themselves to fund raising. One of the most visible and successful has been the Welcome House Thrift Shop. Primarily organized by Lois Burpee and Muriel Beister, the shop continues, now directed by daughter-in-law Elizabeth Beister. The role the shop plays in publicizing Welcome House, or in continuing financial support, has been considerable. It is one more example of the generous contributions made by dedicated supporters of Welcome House.

In the final analysis, it must be concluded that Doylestown, like the smaller communities of Dublin and Blooming Glen, served diligently and purposefully as vital forces that made Welcome House. Though my feelings here are drawn more from impressions rather than from constant interaction, as in Blooming Glen and Dublin, I am nonetheless just as convinced of their positive contributions to Welcome House—good people yielding good results.

The words of Pearl Buck, written in the *Green Hills News*, July 1951, provide an appropriate conclusion to the community analysis:

> *We began two and one-half years ago with two children and one house. . . . The idea was a new one to our community. Few people knew how difficult a time children of Asian-born ancestry, though born in America and, therefore, American*

citizens, have in the United States. . . . Social agencies usually find it impossible to place these American-born children in adoptive homes, either American or Asian. . . . I would not have dared to suggest that these children live in our community except that I have found less prejudice here than in almost any other part of the United States. At any rate, the two children who began Welcome House were brought to me, with the hope that something could be done, and I turned to other members of the community for cooperation. The response has been generous, and this in itself has been, for me, a source of new faith in my own country and our people.

These are the sentiments I have tried to capture. The good hearts that were so apparently present in the communities combined with the generous support from church and school, provided the necessary milieu for the unusual social experience to flourish. From one who traveled through these years and witnessed much of what happened, I can truly report it was a happy journey.

Chapter 10

THE RESULTS

The permanent and far-reaching impact of Welcome House was aptly demonstrated for me five years ago while visiting in Chapel Hill, North Carolina. My brother-in-law had met a young physical therapist in the University of North Carolina Hospital and discovered that she was a Welcome House adoptee. He surprised her with his knowledge of Welcome House. Since I was his source of information, he suggested she speak to me. She was quite eager to do so; consequently, a meeting was arranged. It was a most delightful afternoon.

The vagaries of life were revealed here. Had she been born a year or two earlier, she most likely would have been my sister. But instead she was one of the first Welcome House children to be placed in an adoptive home. She told me about her life. By coincidence, she grew up very close to Albright College, and then moved to Ohio. She thinks of herself as having a very normal, happy life. She was raised in a religious family where her father was a minister. Well educated, she acquired both a college and professional degree. She combines a married and professional life with quite obvious success. At the time we spoke, she was about to have her first child. In her opinion, the Welcome House system made it all possible. Her personal story is one among many.

The Asiatic-American has become part of our American culture. Other personal examples illustrate this point. Over ten years ago, a candidate for an Albright College administrative position arrived on campus for an interview. In the course of his visit, he talked of his family. Three of his children were adopted through Welcome House. Welcome House children had reached as far as his native

Iowa. Two faculty colleagues are the adoptive parents of Asian-Americans. It is hard to imagine these two families without the joy that comes through the gentle presence of the child and loving care of the parents—truly matches made in heaven.

Also, a few months ago I was asked to talk about the Welcome House story at a local service club dinner. After my remarks, one of the members stopped by my table. He explained that his son had adopted a child through Welcome House, and he warmly reported the family experience. The proud grandfather saw the child, not as an Asian orphan, but as a totally loved and typical grandchild. He, too, was grateful for Welcome House; his obvious joy made me feel especially good. And most recently a student in my evening class at Albright happily informed me that he and his wife had been approved as adoptive parents by Welcome House. They will soon be happy parents; just one more example of the coincidental but widespread impact of Welcome House.

Though I may be more conscious of the phenomenon of Asians in American life due to my Welcome House past, the increasing presence of this minority group is undeniable. In addition to the above, I would include an Asian wife of a lunch-counter friend, Asian friends of my children, Asian students in my class and on my tennis team, Asian colleagues, Asian bank tellers—the list goes on.

Random examples of the changing life for Asian-Americans offers insight into the new pattern of American minority life. But the statistical growth of Asian-Americans in this country is greater proof of the shifting status. The Immigration Act of 1965 was crucial in bringing about this growth. With that act, Congress abolished the National origins quota system of the 1920s, a system that was so discriminating against Asians. Though still limiting immigration to 170,000 persons outside the western hemisphere, the new Act admits non-westerners on a first-come, first-served basis. With this new formula, immigration policies improved during the subsequent decades. Also, in 1975,

Congress created a Select Commission on Immigration and Refugee Policy. Specific Congressional action constantly increased the refugee and immigrant numbers. Asian immigration benefited the most from this changing climate. From virtual exclusion during and after the 1920s, Asians have become the leading immigration group from non-Western countries. Today, Asian-Americans are proportionately the fastest growing minority group in the United States, with an increase between 1970 and 1980 of 143 percent.

By contrast, Latino immigration increased by thirty-eight percent in the same decade. In 1960, there were 877,934 Asians in the United States. In 1990, the Asian population exceeded 7,200,000. Between 1970 and 1990, the Asian population tripled while the general population increased by thirty-four percent. It is estimated that Asians will make up four percent of the U.S. population by the year 2000.

In addition, the ethnic studies of Larry Shinagawa, a professor of Asian-American studies at Sonoma State University, point out some important changes for Asians in American life. Concentrating on the Asian population of California, Professor Shinagawa examined California marriage records, conducted interviews, and surveyed racial attitudes. He has uncovered some remarkable statistics. More than thirty-five percent of all Asians in California marry interracially. Even more significantly, seventy percent of all U.S.-born Asians of California between the ages of twenty-five and forty marry outside their race. With an identified average of 2.2 children per mixed marriage, it is clear that a multi-racial society is emerging. Though California is the statistical leader in this pattern, Professor Shinagawa estimates that ten percent of the national Asian population will marry interracially. One can only conclude that there is an inexorable march toward a multicultural America in these observations.

The random examples and the brief statistical commentary indicate that a remarkable transformation has been underway. The earlier national policies of exclusion, restriction, incarceration, discrimination, and violence have been overturned or muted. The awful stereotypes of the "dirty Jap" is history for most Americans. Many of my students had never heard the stereotype until studying World War II. In fact, many Americans now think of Japanese-Americans as the "model minority." Their achievement, along with other Asians, has won them respect as they succeed in academia in the arts, sports, and business. Though racism has not been eradicated, life for Asian-Americans today, in no way, resembles the discriminatory ways of yesteryear.

How did this happen? Much of the credit goes to the dedication and resourcefulness of determined Asian cultures. Japanese, Vietnamese, Korean, and other Asians have come to these shores with a purpose, and have successfully pursued their goals. Still, American attitudes toward Asians had to change if this were to happen. And for this, the influence of Welcome House was essential.

This became particularly true as the Welcome House system developed beyond the home and family of my parents. In 1951, Welcome House added something new to its child placement policies. The Yoder family was nearly complete, but more children needed to be placed. Couples seeking to adopt still had not considered an Asian baby. It was another moment of decision in Welcome House history. As a consequence, Pearl Buck began what she had vowed to do—establish as many families as necessary to take care of the children. Thus, another home, Welcome House II, as it was frequently called, came into being.

The minutes of the Welcome House Board for April 25, 1961, document the decision to open a new home. According to the minutes, Mr. and Mrs. Henry Ruth of Lansdale, Pennsylvania, were unanimously chosen to be the new parents. The board minutes noted that the Ruths were highly recommended by the Yoders.

Welcome House II was to end Pearl Buck's campaign to create families for the unwanted Asian-American child.

It wasn't that there were no more children to place. Rather, by the end of 1953, the Asian-American children had become adoptable. After a long struggle, Mrs. Walsh and her supporters had successfully challenged the convention that matched children with parents by biological compatability. No longer were hair or eye color a necessary match; and now, no longer was similar race even a requirement. In a world that calls for equality among all people, no matter what the race or creed, this seems a proper end. And for many thousands, as we shall see, this policy brought happiness and opportunity.

Part of the Welcome House mission from its very inception was to explore the adoption possibilities for Asian children. A separate office was created and served as a focal point for all Welcome House needs. In a small summer kitchen on the farm of David and Lois Burpee, the staff (secretary, social worker, volunteers) fulfilled its pioneering role with distinction. It paid the bills, organized fund raising, and identified new children in need of homes. Within this setting, the adoption process was gradually formulated. However, it was emphasized that no Yoder or Ruth children were available for adoption. (In those early years, many had asked to adopt a number of my brothers and sisters.) The Welcome House Board, under Pearl Buck's leadership, was adamant in maintaining the permanence of the families they had started. Adoption was a second and distinctively separate step. And so, Welcome House discovered what needed to be done in this new and difficult area of child placement.

As Pearl Buck stated in one of her books, *Children for Adoption*,

> *As the focus of Welcome House shifted more to adoption, our efforts kept broadening—again simply because of necessity. Other agencies turned to us for help in finding homes for various types of hard-to-place children. Though originally chartered to care for any child who needs our help, we have placed many handicapped*

children in loving homes. Of course, no agency any-
where has sufficient funds to solve the total problem
of children in need. The only alternative is to help
child by child, and that is what we propose to do.

Lois Burpee reported that originally most of the
work was done by board members and volunteers. Then,
in 1952, Richard Steinman was hired as executive director.
He and Pearl Buck had the job of studying each family and
home in order to make a placement decision. He reported
their method. "When we get a request for a child, we sub-
mit that inquiry to three tests: 1) why is the family asking
for a child; 2) will this be a good place for a child to be; and
3) which will be the best child to give to this individual
family?" The results of these early efforts can be evaluated
in a number of ways.

To begin with, consider the growth. It was in 1951
that Welcome House first found adoptive homes for the
Asian-American children. That year, six children were
placed with different adoptive families. Between 1951 and
1960, 153 children were placed. During the fifties, all the
children were Amerasian, but born in this country. After
1960, children from foreign countries were also adopted
through Welcome House. This was in keeping with the
Welcome House charter revision of 1953 that increased the
adoption option for Welcome House from Asian-Americans
born in the United States, to any hard-to-place child regard-
less of birthplace. With an expanded pool of children and
increased acceptance of the racially, or ethnically-mixed
family, Welcome House has had the following success: 1961
to 1970—856 adoptions; 1971 to 1980—2,236 adoptions: 1981
to 1990—1,948 adoptions. The grand total exceeds 5,200
adoptions during these four decades. The benefits to these
adopted children is obvious.

However, the value of Welcome House goes beyond
the children. All of us benefit from an increased sense of
tolerance and understanding. Each who are touched by the
Welcome House experience have a heightened awareness

of human diversity and new insights into cultural pluralism. That was the message spread by the network that surrounded Welcome House, be it the national celebrity or financier, or the local supporter and friends. And other, more formal structures, also developed.

For example, early in the adoption history, the adoptive parents formed a loose amalgamation of concerned families, convinced they needed support and protection for their new children in a society uncomfortable with interracial adoption. During the 1950s, they met at the home of Pearl Buck for potluck picnics and sharing information. As numbers increased, the meeting place moved from the Pearl Buck living room to the recreation center in the Buck barn, and finally, weather permitting, to the lawn.

By the early 1960s, the group had named itself The Welcome House Adoptive Parents Association. A mimeographed newsletter was sent three or four times per year to 238 member families. In 1965, the name was changed to Welcome House Adoptive Parents Group and incorporation plans were started.

By 1967, WHAPG developed interests beyond the immediate problems and needs of the members. For example, it worked to relieve the sufferings of Vietnamese orphans. Thousands of dollars were eventually raised and donated for Vietnamese relief. This interest in international aid was also carried on through a program known as Partners in Caring (PIC). Individual children who could not leave the foreign country were sponsored by annual financial support. Over 600 children have been sponsored by Partners In Caring.

News of Welcome House, the Welcome House Adoptive Parents Group, and Partners in Caring is now shared through *The Welcomer*. The mimeographed newsletter, originally for 250 families, had become a well-crafted organ with professional personnel and typeset copies and photographs. Its mailing list includes 6,400 names, and its message supports the type of concerns that have always been part of the Welcome House system.

As WHAPG President Janet Plangenman wrote in 1989, "WHAPG is an active organization of some twenty independent adoptive parent groups and numerous individuals throughout New Jersey, Pennsylvania, Delaware, Virginia, and North Carolina, and annual dues support Partners in Caring and *The Welcomer*. While WHAPG raises money for Welcome House's support of needy children overseas, the individual chapters also take on many very worthy projects themselves. These projects range from donating adoption books to community libraries, to sponsoring overseas orphanages. WHAPG continues to believe in helping the children left behind and cooperates with Welcome House in that effort."

And so it can be concluded that the Welcome House adoptive system, with its surrounding support groups, continues to fulfill the original purpose of Pearl Buck and my parents—the needs of unfortunate children are being addressed. True, the method is different, but the compassion, love, and financial support that brings happiness and life to thousands, is an end that all of the original organizers of Welcome House would applaud.

Other organizations have paralleled the Welcome House work. Beginning in the 1950s, Pearl Buck and the Welcome House staff advised other adoption agencies about the problems and methods for interracial adoption. With this counsel, and with the obvious need, these agencies also participated in interracial adoption. By increasing the numbers of participants in this process, these agencies became another source for breaking down the earlier prejudices against Asians and improving the quality of life for unfortunate children. Rita James Sunion and Howard Altstein report that, in addition to Welcome House, Social Services of America, Travelers Aid International, Catholic Relief Service, Friends of All Children, and Holt Adoption Program have been actively involved in locating American families for Asian children. And the two sociologists also indicate that though no exact figures exist, more than 100,000 Korean children alone have been adopted by

Western families since 1950. The trickle of help for Asian-American children had become a fast-moving stream.

In 1964, Pearl Buck added a new method for helping unfortunate, unwanted children. She started the Pearl S. Buck Foundation. The Foundation reflects the lifelong interest of its founder; its purpose was aptly captured in its mission statement. The goal is

> to foster cross-cultural understanding and to help children around the world who have been displaced through mixed heredity, amid conflict, hunger, poverty, or other circumstances. The Foundation's mission is to give these children the opportunity to develop to their fullest potential and to become self-sufficient, productive citizens.

The children that the Foundation has aided over the last twenty-five years have been primarily offspring of American soldiers and Asian women, first in Korea and then Vietnam. The Foundation was necessary, according to Pearl Buck, because Welcome House and other agencies were focused on placement and adoption within American families in this country. The new Foundation would emphasize the need to help Asian-Americans in the Asian countries. This was done because it was our responsibility to help the children of illegitimate birth that had no father and little, if any, financial support. And they needed this support in their own country.

The Foundation had some early controversy surround it. To begin with, Pearl Buck surprised her good friend, Margaret Fischer, with the first public announcement of her plans. Mrs. Fischer told me that Pearl Buck was to be honored in January 1964 with the prestigious Gimbel Award for Humanity. The winner was not publicly announced before the award luncheon, but Mrs. Fischer attended the event, strongly suspecting that Pearl Buck would be chosen. Consequently, the official selection of Pearl Buck for the award was no surprise, but her winner's acceptance speech certainly was. As Pearl Buck rose to receive the award, Mrs. Fischer was thrilled for her friend; she also assumed the $1,000 cash portion of the honor would become a valuable addition to the Welcome House budget for the year. She was shocked when Pearl Buck announced that the $1,000 would be the first donation for the Pearl S. Buck Foundation, a new foundation for orphans who could not leave the country of their birth. Korean War orphans were the primary examples at that moment.

Mrs. Fischer was totally taken back by the announcement. There were some rumors of a new foundation, yet nothing concrete had been discussed. Like Mrs. Fischer, the entire Welcome House Board was shaken. None were certain what consequences the new foundation would have on Welcome House, or what Pearl Buck would do regarding Welcome House. The Board minutes of April capture this uncertainty. At that meeting the Board president suggested it would be helpful to have Mrs. Walsh describe the new foundation. She presented a general background for her actions. The foundation was "to care for children who cannot leave the countries of their birth." She also assured the Board that there would be no conflict of interest between the two foundations, and no conflict over solicitation of funds. She announced that she would be the president and treasurer; Martin Snyder of Fidelity Philadelphia Trust would be the secretary; Theodore Harris, formerly of Arthur Murray Studio, would be executive secretary.

It was the last appointment that created the most controversy. Mrs. Fischer explained that earlier Ted Harris had been denied a seat on the Welcome House Board of Directors. His qualifications were questioned. Unrecorded, but perhaps more importantly, he may have been rejected because some felt his association with Pearl Buck was improper. He had come into her life in the period after her husband's death.

According to friends and family, at that time she was pursuing various ways to keep busy with new and interesting activities. I know about a few of her new interests. For example, she asked my wife to give her French lessons.

On another occasion, on a warm summer afternoon, while sitting by her swimming pool, she spoke to me about sports for over an hour. As I remember, we covered a wide range of topics—from sports stars to the great teams of the past. She asked my opinion about the value of sports in life. Her own feelings, as always, were insightful and ahead of her time. She observed that the sports world needed to pay more attention to women athletes and their rights, if the sports institution was to live up to its claim as a training ground for living. It was a surprising afternoon, because she knew a great deal about sports and spoke with interest and authority, a part of her I had never before experienced. In truth, I had always felt that her main justification for athletics was for physical conditioning. Of course, she still believed this, but now she proved to have another dimension—that of a knowledgeable fan. This was just one more of the activities she was cultivating. But there were others. She took swimming and diving lessons, and she turned to ballroom dancing. Clearly, this was a seventy-two-year-old widow searching for different life experiences.

Ballroom dancing turned out to be her most significant new venture. Nora Stirling, in her biography of Pearl Buck, describes it this way. "A message to the Arthur Murray Dance Studio in Jenkintown said, 'My daughters need to be taught the social dances. Please send a teacher.'"

Theodore Findley Harris was the teacher who arrived on July 5, 1963.

> *Red-headed, pale, with a dancer's walk and an actor's precise diction, he entered the house and looked around. In a flash he had taken in the grounds, the wealthy elderly woman with foreign-looking daughters, and no man in sight. . . . In a week, Harris had skimmed through her books and, while filing away her answers to his flattering questions, learned her history, her tastes, her philanthropies.*

Pearl Buck was completely overwhelmed by the youthful charm and the enthusiasm of the thirty-two-year-old instructor. His ideas flowed quickly and easily. At first,

Welcome House was to be the recipient of his flair for fund raising. Charity balls, in keeping with his abilities, were the first option. It began in October 1963 in the Pearl Buck barn. The ball raised $700 and was celebrated as a great success. Astonished friends watched as Pearl Buck waltzed through the evening in the arms of her dance instructor.

Plans now skyrocketed. Convention Hall in Philadelphia was targeted for the second ball. That still was to be a Welcome House benefit, but a shift of Foundation allegiance was underway, prompted in part, no doubt, by the Welcome House Board's rejection of Harris as a member.

With some apparent hope that the two agencies would eventually become one, Pearl Buck and Harris planned the gala charity ball. As an official Welcome House fund raiser, the event was a social and financial success. Dorothy Kilgallen served as mistress of ceremony; Sophie Tucker and Johnny Ray provided singing entertainment. Again, Pearl Buck displayed her dancing talents, sharing the floor with her attentive teacher. The event raised $13,000 and was widely reported by the press. Letters in the program from Lady Bird Johnson and Robert Kennedy indicate the public regard for Pearl Buck and her accomplishments. Mrs. Johnson writes, "No words could be as moving and as great a tribute to you as the wonderful work you have initiated at Welcome House. . . . The President joins me in expressing immeasurable pride in your accomplishments. . . ." Robert Kennedy writes, "The work of Welcome House is a treasure of riches—providing homes for the lost and unprotected child and reaching across the divisible lines of race and nation. . . ."

With this success, Pearl Buck was further convinced that the talented young dancer was the proper choice to lead her new Foundation. They turned to other projects. Fund raising through massive letter writing was an early step. Based on her name and literary achievements, many luminaries joined the movement. The Foundation letterhead in 1965 included the following: Steve Allen, Rear Admiral Philip Ashler, Art Buchwald, Joan Crawford, General

Dwight Eisenhower, Arlene Francis, Huntington Hartford III, Robert Kennedy, Gypsy Rose Lee, Joseph Levine, Mrs. William Scranton, R. Sargent Shriver, Sophie Tucker, Fred Waring, General James Van Fleet, Princess Grace of Monaco, the Ambassador of Korea to the United States, and the Ambassador of the United States to Korea (both listed by title, but not by name).

Many personal letters followed. With her humanitarian interests, and the message of little children in need, her appeal was always well received. A national tour of twenty-two charity balls was put into the schedule. It was a major undertaking; but it was a fund-raising blitz that was marked for success. And the beneficiary of this extravaganza was to be the Pearl Buck Foundation. Welcome House was lost in the shuffle.

At this point a personal observation seems in order. Pearl Buck's participation in my parents' Welcome House was coming to a conclusion. Perhaps properly, her vision had broadened and she felt the need to address a larger problem—the world's neglected children. At any rate, after 1965, she stopped actively being the grandmother for my brothers and sisters. Her once regular visits to Welcome House ended. True, all the children were at the teenage and young adult stages of their lives and probably needed her less. Yet, at the time, it seemed quite strange. In fact, our only contact during the last eight years of Pearl Buck's life was a kind sympathy note sent to Mother when Dad died; a note to Mother after Jack, my brother, was killed in a car accident; and her eightieth birthday party in 1972 where Mother, Sumi, Leon, and Paul attended. Her note after Jack's tragic accident indicates the distance that had developed between the grandmother and her grandchildren.

Danby, Vermont
July 10, 1971

My Dear Mrs. Yoder:

 Last night Jean called me to tell me of the tragic death of Jack. This morning Mrs. Burpee called. I am overwhelmed by the tragic events in this young life. I keep remembering him as he came to us, a little baby. It has been one of the regrets of my life that I have not known him and the other Welcome House children better as they grew up. It would have been a joy. But I did not want to press the matter. I told them when I saw them, which was rarely, that they were always welcome to come to see me, use the barn, swimming pool, tennis court, etc. After that, I had to leave it to them to do what they wished. Now, of course, I think of you. You have had so much to bear of recent years that I do feel for you deeply. I am glad that Dale and his family are back, and of course Charlotte is with you, a strong help always, I know—as my Jean is to me. You must remember that you and Mr. Yoder did all you could for Jack. You gave him a family, a loving home, and above all, a father and mother—none of which he had. Of course, I know that he could never have recovered fully from the shock of the previous accident and for this we cannot blame him. My thoughts are constantly with you.

> *Your affectionate friend,*
> *Pearl S. Walsh*

The sympathy extended was appreciated. Her condolences were undoubtedly sincere. But some of the conflict in her life is in the message. She had to feel the distance that her new life had created. The offer to use her recreational facilities had always been honored. The children continued to use the swimming pool, and on occasion the barn and tennis court. But Pearl Buck wasn't there when they were, and, of course, as stated earlier, she never came to Welcome House after 1965.

Expecting the children to somehow initiate the contact with her was very unrealistic. My own evaluation of the letter would be that she felt an obligation to respond to Jack's death and mourned the loss of the young life. Jack was someone who was greatly loved, a person of gentle demeanor and quiet style. He had suffered a grievous loss in the accident referred to in the letter. His high school girlfriend was killed in a car accident and Jack had continued to suffer emotional distress over that loss. Having made the contact for very compassionate reasons, Mrs. Walsh also had to somehow account for the virtual vacuum that had developed over the previous six years. By reminding us of the offer to the children, she shifted responsibility, and I suppose, exonerated herself in her own mind.

How does one explain this abrupt shift in spirit and action? Undoubtedly, the demands of the new Foundation were consuming and significant, and her interest in eliminating the suffering of the world's children was certainly noble and beyond criticism. But her loss of interest in the Welcome House grandchildren was not. Many of her friends and associates noted the change in her. For most, the only logical explanation was Ted Harris. His power over her was seen by friends and family as strange and compelling. Yet, how could one of America's most admired woman be so controlled by a "poorly educated social climber who lived by his wits and his feet"? Here are some of the explanations that Nora Stirling discovered: "She was plain lonely;" "It was his youth;" "It could be plain sex;" "She needed an escort and a sounding board for ideas;" "It was a mother-son thing;" "When she danced with him she was flying through the air;" "He treated her like a princess, took her back to her Nobel days." And so the list goes.

An exposé by the *Philadelphia Magazine* in July 1969 adds credence to this position. Harris is portrayed as the opportunistic con-man who led the elderly woman down an unfortunate path with a power that was all-consuming. Disclosures of Harris's impropriety in use of funds (cars, boats, swimming pools, a personal cook, etc.) were met with angry denials by Mrs. Walsh. His public displays of foot-stamping or shrill abuse toward people who might question his authority meant little to her. Such public tirades that friends thought should have embarrassed her were dismissed with her explanation that he was "very brilliant, very high-strung, and artistic."

But the extravagant lifestyle was too easy to observe. My mother and other staff members of Mrs. Walsh

witnessed the apparent spending binge even before the rev-
elations of *Philadelphia Magazine.* The Harrises' weekend
hideaway, a wonderful old farmhouse near Welcome
House, was undergoing many changes. An expensive boat
was towed to the house; a swimming pool was installed.
Carpenters and painters seemed to be constantly on the
estate. The conclusion seemed simple; much money was
being spent to improve the part-time home of the Foundation director.

Now powerful figures also became curious. Dr.
Richard Wilson of Arizona, as a Foundation board member
and as a million-dollar donor, decided to investigate. He
didn't like what he found. The Korean operation was
grossly undersupported. Many administrators had resigned
and called for changes, but no concerns had reached Pearl
Buck. Charges of sexual misconduct by Harris with male
teenagers, who were brought to the Harris rural home, were
apparently confirmed. (One of the young men also told a
Pennridge teacher about this situation.)

An audit of the Foundation's finances produced
evidence of total chaos. It was impossible to understand
how much money had been taken in, or how it had been
spent. The end result was the resignation of Harris on July
7, 1969. He disappeared immediately and was never
charged with any crime. Pearl Buck defended him and dismissed the report. She saw this as "smut publicity" and a
serious attack on the Foundation. Her loyalty to Ted Harris
was such that she eventually formed another Foundation
with him in Danby, Vermont—this one for "creative artists."

But this sad episode has a happy ending that really
is another beginning. The Foundation, left in such disar-
ray, righted itself. Initially, the Pennsylvania Commission
on Charitable Organizations accepted the charges of financial mismanagement and revoked the Foundation's license.
However, new leadership and reformed procedures resulted in a reissued license, and the Foundation was back
in business. Its recovery was slow, but constant hard work
and planning brought the agency the kind of praise and

success it deserved, considering its noble purpose. Grace Sum, a past executive director, told me that over 25,000 Amerasians throughout East Asia have been helped with food, medicine, and education.

The "new beginning" continued with the merger of The Pearl Buck Foundation and Welcome House in October 1991. The program that Pearl Buck envisioned before she became so tragically side-tracked is now in place. On her own homestead, her dream is being fulfilled. Her love and compassion for the unloved is being carefully nurtured and continued by a caring and trained staff. And the growth continues.

For the past three years, Executive Director Meredith Richardson has led the Foundation, which continues its mission to serve needy children and their families. Children in Vietnam, Korea, China, Romania, Russia, Thailand, the Philippines, and the United States have received loving support granted through H.E.L.P.+ The acronym stands for Health, Education, Livelihood, and Psycho-social development. The + is added to indicate that adoption is a possibility when a family or community can no longer care for a child. With these stated goals, the Foundation has increased its ways to help the impoverished, the orphaned, the disabled, the homeless, or the sick child. Currently the Foundation reaches about 25,000 children annually, a statistic that reveals that more and more needy children are being helped through dedicated efforts of the Foundation.

Also, in 1999 one more step was taken in the long journey that began fifty years earlier when tiny, unwanted David became the first child of Welcome House. For clarification, the Foundation has changed its name to Pearl S. Buck International, Inc. As a new century approaches, it is thrilling to contemplate that a single child who started this movement has been replaced by virtually hundreds of thousands. One small step started a journey.

Thus, the Welcome House system, begun so long ago by my parents, has evolved into a carefully constructed process that provides better lives for Asian-Americans in ways never predicted. In turn, others have accepted the Welcome House-type philosophy and the nationwide change for Asian-Americans, as we have seen, has been phenomenal. Again, I repeat, Welcome House was not the only reason for this remarkable shift, but it was the beginning. The rural family in the isolated village has left its mark, and for that impact, I give credit to my parents.

Though the results are commendable, they do conflict with historical tradition, both in this country and elsewhere. As Arthur Schlesinger, Jr. has written: "The hostility of one tribe for another is among the most instinctive human reactions." Instead of Welcome House-style integration, the world has had wars, enslavement, genocide, apartheid, segregation, ethnic cleansing, lynching, and the like. It is a most odious record and one that threatens us all. And with the ending of the Cold War, it has gotten worse.

In many countries, internal conflicts have erupted among racial and ethnic groups formerly united by a common enemy or dictatorial control. As Schlesinger points out, "ethnicity is the cause of the breaking of nations," witness the Soviet Union, Yugoslavia, India, South America, Sri Lanka, Burma, Ethiopia, Indonesia, Iraq, . . . "The virus of tribalism risks becoming the aids of international politics." Even Canada, one of the five richest nations in the world, a place where "the world's poor are beating at the door to get in," is threatening to come apart over ethnic differences. Such observations are sobering and promise a bleak future if not positively addressed and solved.

Can the spirit that made Welcome House such a local success somehow invade the large context of ethnic and racial rivalry and help solve this awful dilemma? Again, it would be both grandiose and simplistic to make such a claim. The problem is too large, too complex, and too ingrained to eliminate with a simple call for love, tolerance, and understanding of all racial and ethnic groups.

Racism is still too easily identified. Also, some cultural pluralists emphasize the need for ethnic or racial identity, sometimes to the detriment of the nation as a whole. When the multi-culturalists produce pride, love, or respect for traditions, and strong, committed group members, their efforts are laudable. When they produce inaccurate assessments of the past, false evaluation of current practices, or emotional rejection of all that is outside their interests, their efforts are little more than reverse racism. The ideals of Welcome House hold little value for such individuals. So is there any way to overcome the ravages of the racists or ethnocentric inaccuracies of some multi-culturalists? Perhaps.

To begin with, the sad reality of past and present racism can be contrasted to an optimistic reduction of race relations that more closely parallels the Welcome House concept of integration. From this perspective, blatant racism has been under attack in this country for a long time. Slavery is gone. The Second Reconstruction has filled the legal mechanisms that defended second-class citizenship. Norman Grabner, distinguished Professor of History at the University of Virginia, stated in a bicentennial lecture in 1976, that he was proud to acknowledge that in the year of celebration, "all citizens were at last equal before the law of the land." He was probably correct from a purely legal standpoint. And certainly we have come a great distance from the days of slavery. For instance, could any public figure offer the following?

> *I will say now that I am not, nor ever have been, in favor of bringing about in any way the social and political equality of the white and the black races, and inasmuch as they cannot so live, while they remain together there must be the position of superior and inferior, and I, as much as any man, am in favor of having the superior position assigned to the white race.*

Certainly not. But the Great Emancipator did in 1858. And two years later, he was President of the United States.

David Duke and Louis Farrakan have discovered, from different sides of the race question, that racism and anti-Semitism cannot be part of a national platform. Open advocacy of these despicable goals will not be rewarded by general public support, although we know there is still historical residue of these awful isms. But the point is, we have made identifiable strides in the face of the lingering irrationality. We have elected an Irish Catholic as President; we have had Jewish, black, and women governors and national leaders; and formerly restricted social clubs have accepted minority members. Some claim this to be the tip of an iceberg that continues to have defacto, if not dejure, limits on minorities throughout the submerged mass of the ice metaphor. It is difficult to dispute this in the face of statistics revealing black-white differences in education, prison populations, illegitimate children, and the like. Defacing Jewish synagogues, attacking Asian shopkeepers, and belittling Latinos, add substances to charge that little has changed.

Thus, what we conclude about the current condition of racism is still subject to interpretation. However, the history of bi-racial and bi-ethnic growth is more empirical. True, the melting pot metaphor is more rhetorical than actual, but we have always honored the ideal as a goal to reach. Ralph Waldo Emerson saw our populations as a "smelting pot," with people being "a new compound more precious than any." Herman Melville wrote, "You cannot spill a drop of American blood without spilling the blood of the whole world." Others, such as George Washington, John Quincy Adams, St. John de Crevecoeur, Alexis de Trequiville, James Bryce, Frederick Jackson Turner, Henry James, and others, saw an emerging new "race" of Americans blended from the many ethnic and cultural groups that came to our shores. Even Gunner Myrdal, who wrote so convincingly of American failures in treating the black minority, emphasized what he called the "American Creed," that is, Americans "of all national origins, regions, creeds, and colors," holding "the most explicitly expressed system of general ideals," of any country in the western world.

This evidence establishes a traditional base of cultural assimilation. Recent evidence suggests that the melting pot ideal is coming to fruition in many ways. Diane Ravitch explains this trend in an interesting way. She states, "Paradoxical though it may seem, the United States has a common culture that is multicultural." This "multicultural common culture" began with earlier examples. The Irish-Catholic President, the studies of Professor Shinagawa, and, of course, Welcome House are followed by other evidence in contemporary times. Since 1970, interracial marriages have tripled, from 310,000 in 1970 to 1,195,000 in 1993. These couples and the children of these marriages have developed a "multicultural" interest group. They have developed biracial campus groups (Prism at Harvard, Spectrum at Stanford), books (*Black, White,* others), magazines (*New People* and *Interace*), and support groups.

There is a movement to put a "multiracial" category on the next census. Nancy Brown is white and married to an African-American. After she discovered her children had no social designation, she co-founded Multiracial Americans of Southern California. She is quoted: "It is very hurtful to be told your child has to identify with one race when there are two participants in the union. It can be psychologically damaging to kids not to be able to claim who they really are."

The biracial question was addressed by *Ebony* magazine in an article titled, "Who's Black and Who's Not?" According to the article, it is not the increasing number of children from mixed parents, but the denial of heritage for economic, social, or career gain. Jennifer Beals, Nenet Cherry, Sade, Irene Cura, Rae Dawn Chong, Lenny Kravitz, and Roland Gift were criticized for downplaying their racial backgrounds. Perhaps a twelve-year-old reader's response gets to the heart of the matter. Ebonee Warren wrote to the editor and admonished the author for putting "too much emphasis on black and white. I am one-quarter black, one-quarter Seminole Indian, and one-half white, and this is exactly what I tell people when they ask about my color. . . . We are biracial and proud of it."

Also, Carlos Fernandez of the Association of Multi-Ethnic Americans comments insightfully: "We're all going to be a minority, so we are all going to have to cooperate with each other. Hopefully, the cultures that make up this country will contribute to a new fusion."

Welcome House produced a local mindset that accepted the racially different child. Perhaps the national mindset can grow and mature. What has emerged over the last decades is the legal framework for equality, accompanied by the acceptance of equality from certain peoples. But the entire nation must recognize its responsibility and support the effort to achieve cultural diversity. The goal must be to allow the ethnic and racial minority an individualized sense of identity and dignity mixed with the unconditional opportunity to participate in the broad institutional life of America. Some have called this reverse racism. But, based upon the centuries of discrimination and our American belief in freedom, it seems this is a legitimate correction.

There is some evidence that suggests this can be accomplished. The aforementioned attitudes that recognize the civil rights of racial and ethnic groups must be adopted by all. The changes in attitudes toward Asians must be increased and extended to all racial groups.

Positive self worth, greater respect, intermarriage—all have been identified and suggest that Asians have found their way into American society.

The example of Welcome House serves this end very well, in my opinion. A means for accepting the racially different person with little resistance was set in motion. And by this precedent, one can hope for similar success on a larger scale. Perhaps Dr. Pangloss is again raising his head here, but hope and persistent effort are formidable traits. The Pearl Buck legacy continues through the efforts of the good people of the Pearl Buck/Welcome House Foundation. Their goal of achieving love and tolerance on this "good earth" is an admirable one. Hopefully, it will extend to everyone, no matter the cultural or ethnic past.

— *Chapter 11* —

SOME REFLECTIONS

The preceding chapters have revealed the success-ful growth and development of an unusual family. Church, school, and community accepted a family of remarkable makeup and, contrary to tradition or conventional wisdom, the arrangement flourished. Credit has been assigned for this pioneering social experience, but it seems to me some specific reflections are vital in completing this tale. There is no way to measure the many specific contributions of individuals and arrive at some rank order of importance for the success of Welcome House. But no one could question the obvious conclusion that my parents were the most important reason for the family's success. Their commitment is the type of action too rarely taken in an apathetic society. To give a portion of one's wealth or to volunteer a portion of one's time for a worthy cause is deserving of praise. But to give one's entire life deserves the keys to the kingdom.

Both my parents were unusual people. Mother, with a limited formal education, but a high level of innate intelligence, was able to subvert herself to a life of committed service. In today's age of rising expectations and deserving recognition of equality for women (which I fully support), Mother's life was more traditionally tied to hearth and home. But what Mother accomplished was hardly traditional. True, she practiced some of the old ideals. Her children had to be spotlessly clean. Washing and ironing clothing were part of her daily routine (she even ironed the underwear). Her cleanliness emphasis has resulted in a whole family of neatniks (except for one), but I guess that's not so bad. Church and patriotism were also high on her list. And in proper and fair perspective, these can be accepted as well. She believed in honesty and fairness and kindness. But most of all, she believed and practiced love. She loved us all.

Although Mother was traditional in training and action, she was modern enough to recognize the changing times. She accepted the new ideas of life and politics. She even changed her own politics, and in looking back with great fondness on John Kennedy and the Democratic Party's goals, she wondered aloud how the Republicans ever captured her loyalty. She also realized that changing times meant new gender assignments as well. She expressed great pride in all her children's achievements and gloried in their career successes, sons and daughters alike. In truth, and with added emphasis, none could have succeeded without her.

Dad was a remarkable person. Born in the right place, with the proper credentials to open the right doors and point him in the right directions, he could have been anything. His abilities were limitless; his personality was matchless. To reverse one of my dad's favorite celebrities, Will Rogers, "I never met a man that didn't like him." His revered status in our small, rural community can be documented in so many ways. At every school reunion or community activity, someone comes to me to identify the important part Dad played in his or her life. The number of times this has happened is beyond calculation. At his funeral in 1967, community people lined up around the entire block outside the funeral home. The funeral director told me he had never experienced such a testimony of grief and affection in his thirty years. When Dad died, one of his close friends said to me, "I don't know how we can live without Poppy (Dad's lifelong nickname)." Truly, he was loved and respected.

Dad's traditions and life were small town. His nickname, Poppy, originated in a way that revealed his ability to get along with people, even those people whose cultural ways were clearly different and not part of the usual environment of a young rural child. The story is as follows: When Dad was about four, the road that passed by the family farm and on into Blooming Glen was being rebuilt. As later explained to me, rocks about two or three times the size of bricks were placed side by side as a foundation, followed by a crushed stone layer, and then covered with oil to hold the road together. The result was a very solid road which has lasted since those days. My grandfather's farm had two large rock-filled fields that had always been difficult to farm. The proximity to the roadwork and presence of the needed road material gave my grandfather the opportunity to end his battle with these fields that yielded little corn or wheat, and turn instead to quarrying the rocks needed for the road base. The crew that built the road happened to be a group of Italian immigrants. Each day their lunch-time meal would be baskets of fresh tomatoes and bread. No one now knows if they washed these vittels down with Italian wine or fresh Blooming Glen water. My dad was apparently attracted to these almost festive lunch breaks. This little four-year-old took an immediate liking to the friendly workers, with one in particular as his favorite. His name was Popi, and since my dad was his constant shadow, everyone began calling the youngster "Little Poppy." It was the endearing name that lasted through his life.

And Little Poppy grew in this environment. Combining farming and quarrying, the Yoder household seemed to thrive. Three brothers and three sisters were all active and contributed much to the family success. But as Dad grew, he developed a desire to go beyond the family business. Therefore, after graduating from Sellersville-Perkasie High School in 1924, he sold his share of the stone quarry to his siblings. He told me the price was $2,000, but I have found no verification of it.

Looking for another way of life, Dad enrolled in Millersville State Normal School in pursuit of a teaching degree. Completing the two-year normal school program then required for teaching certification, he returned to his community, and at age nineteen in the previously described one-room school, his career of community service was underway.

A review of Dad's lifetime of service is important, for it strikes me as a contribution of unbelievable proportion. His time commitment was inhuman. It is amazing to me, as one hears of the negative impact that workaholic husbands have on family life in America, that my dad achieved such an incredible balance. His church work was regular and constant. Virtually every week of his life included some sort of meeting and/or preparation for the Sunday services. His community service was unending, whether it be fundraising for a particular need or back-breaking work on the athletic fields. And, of course, his school efforts were literally Herculean. In the classroom, he was magnificent, always combining his successful philosophy of life with the subject of the day. Originally, his discipline was history; later, in the Pennridge consolidation, he taught general math—but always, he was excellent and popular.

Beyond the classroom, he carried an extracurricular schedule that would turn most to early retirement. His commitment to the athletic program was total. His multiple coaching assignments were filled with a degree of success that made him a well-known name throughout the larger southeast Pennsylvania area. Recently, a regional Hall of Fame was instituted, and Dad was one of the four names selected for charter installation.

In regards to his athletic involvement, coaching was only part of that. He also had to fulfill the position of athletic director. Scheduling contests for both men and women, securing officials, providing equipment—these were some of the duties he added to his busy schedule. In addition, he was the chief of the grounds crew, preparing all the playing fields, leading whomever would help— parents, players, and friends.

But, it didn't end there. Dad was also the director of all the dramatic productions of the school. They were always well received by the community, and considered a major achievement of the high school. In addition, he aided in all the fund drives. An annual magazine sale to help support the sports program, an ad campaign to underwrite the yearbook, the fund drive to build the gym—these were the types of activities that also required his time and energy, as well as other supportive individuals. In truth, his part-time assignments would be considered more than a full-time position in today's school structure. It should also be noted that all of these services were voluntary, without extra pay. All was done well without complaint. Is it any wonder that Dad had an army of friends?

The balance mentioned earlier still prevailed. As good as Dad was for the church, school, and community, he was even better as a father. When I asked Bobby about his own self-indictment as a "bad child," and how he changed, his answer was simple: "Dad, he made me want to be good," he said. Scott came to us as a child with a troubled past. He soon discovered that firmness and love worked. His past faded and he became one of the adjusted, happy Welcome House kids. Each child, in his or her own way, could offer some similar testimony to Dad's ways. I, myself, would add that I always felt that much of his service to the church and school had a dual capacity. For what was valuable for these institutions doubled in its use for me and my brothers and sisters. Yes, Dad was special, and he knew how to serve.

In these and many other ways, our parents fulfilled their obligations to all of the children and all of their friends. They were unique and made this unbelievable family scene thrive. Their ways, their love, and their lives stand as an achievement for all of us to cherish and to attempt to emulate.

Undoubtedly, Pearl Buck and her family must be given a curtain call and a standing ovation in this review. Without Pearl Buck, there would be no Welcome House. She certainly fought the dragon of discrimination in many ways, and her intelligent, gentle, and wise portrayal of the

Asian people throughout all her writing and lectures paved the way for new understanding and tolerance even before America was willing to practice understanding and tolerance. A marvelous, talented woman, Pearl Buck fulfilled her ideal with distinction. Some of the tragedy of her personal life, as captured in print and known by many, need not be repeated here. As I see it, this was part of her declining years brought on by her husband's death and some mistaken judgments and loyalties.

Even though, for all intents and purposes, Pearl Buck withdrew from Welcome House activities in 1965, turning her energies elsewhere into what some have judged to be questionable pursuits, she will always remain for me the altruistic woman who was the driving force that thwarted the awful specter of unwanted children and vicious anti-Asian discrimination.

Certainly, Mr. Walsh was a figure of importance. His very image was grandfatherly, and all the children loved and respected him. An unfortunate stroke in 1957 made him unable to continue a very active life, causing him to remain in the background for the rest of his years. However, he was always "Granddaddy," and offered much wisdom and counsel to the Welcome House experience.

The Walsh children—John, Jean, Edgar, and Richard—were, likewise, involved with all the happenings. The happy times at the Walsh estate—swimming, basketball, television, and the like—both before and after Welcome House, were made even better by these young friends. They, too, shared in the joy of the new children and never seemed resentful or jealous of the time their mother spent on the Welcome House grandchildren. All four were close friends of all the children; but, due to age similarities, they were particularly good friends with Frank, Lillian, and myself.

Janice Walsh, the oldest of the Walsh children, and no longer living at home when Welcome House began, still was involved in the Walsh family discussion. She recalls that all of the family agreed that the needs of the unwanted children must be addressed directly—no hedging and no footdragging. Make the commitment and solve the problem.

The Walsh family also had an ironic development. The parents, who were too old to adopt, later added four new children to the Walsh family, and like their older siblings, they became good friends of the Yoder children. All filled the function of cousins very well and certainly all the Walshes deserve credit for their enthusiastic and loving contribution.

Members of the Welcome House Board have been earlier discussed so I will only repeat a general acclamation of praise and appreciation for all who participated over the years. Some special people require a few words of comment.

Oscar Hammerstein, a charter member of the Welcome House Board, served as its president from 1953 until his death in 1960. His contribution was of great importance. He and his wife Dorothy occasionally stopped by our home to visit, and certainly the family was strengthened by these well-known figures who seemed so accessible and loving. Like Pearl Buck, the Hammerstein voice in the attack on racial discrimination transcended Welcome House activities. As a talented artist and kindhearted, sensitive person, Oscar Hammerstein addressed the issue of racism in much of his work throughout the late 1940s. His popular musicals of that time found ways to attack many of the standard racist judgments of the post World War II world. *South Pacific*, *Flower Drum Song*, and *The King and I* included sensitive and positive portrayals of East Asians and must have caused many people to reflect on their pejorative, racist judgments about Asians and, in numerous cases, reverse their opinions. Like so many, the Hammerstein contribution was immeasurable but overwhelmingly significant.

Also, the Biesters, the Burpees, and the Fischers should be remembered for their early support and life-long involvement with Welcome House. Muriel Biester, Lois

Burpee, and Margaret Fischer provided constant strength for both my mother and Pearl Buck. All were in regular contact with Mother and counseled her on all types of subjects—the children's colds and fevers, best stores for children's clothing, or the best seeds and plants for the garden (Lois Burpee on this one). Also, they were involved in every phase of the Welcome House operation, from thrift shop to adoption. The work would have been impossible without them.

The men were also major figures. Each assumed much responsibility in organizing and fund raising. Kermit Fischer was particularly active, helping the children through the difficult teenage times. Through summer employment at his company, Fischer and Porter, the children were introduced to another component of the real world at a time when each was growing and maturing, needing some additional social interaction. By earning money, meeting new people who had no connection to their own immediate environment (Fischer and Porter was twenty miles away, with few employees who were previously known by any of the Yoders), and by acquiring some independence with money earned, the children were clearly achieving some personal success.

Kermit Fischer didn't simply supply the summer time employment. He constantly checked on the children, both on the job and by his frequent Saturday morning visits at our home. How do you measure such support?

Through the years, others stepped forward. Dr. and Mrs. Jonathan Stamm were directors and great friends. Dad, in particular, was close to Dr. Stamm since they shared many interests from history to sports. My father was given many books by Dr. Stamm, some of which are on my own bookshelves now.

Alice Stockton, Busby Taylor, and Herbert Barness are other names that were regularly identified by my parents for their help. By singling out these names, I must apologize to those not mentioned. As I went off to college and graduate school and started a family of my own, the day-to-day contact between board members and my parents was less known to me. Still, as with all those mentioned above, profound appreciation is felt for all who participated through the years. This is also true, whether the contribution was a board member who regularly gave of time, energy, and money, or a celebrity, as described earlier. The multitudes who have been helped by Welcome House owe much to the dedicated service of so many. It is truly an example of rallying love and devotion.

Finally, a word must be said about my brothers and sisters. As I told them when I began this project, I would not violate their contemporary privacy. My intention was to explain the growth of an unusual social arrangement; analyze and explain its success, and in truth, offer concrete evidence of the virtues of Mother and Dad. Telling tales of childhood seemed innocent and without penalty to the participants. But, spelling out details of the private lives of each seems to go beyond the boundaries of this work. In a general way, I will say that all have found peace, love, and success in this life. True, we have had our share of sorrow, but we have had more than our share of joy.

For those who might be curious, the various occupations in the family include real estate sales, car sales, retired steelworker, forty-year-old college student, mortgage lender, business executive, car inspector, gas company official, farmer, and social worker. For those who keep track of such statistics, it is interesting to note that the twelve children of the Yoders have taken to heart the biblical injunction to go forth and multiply. From eleven married children (Jack died in a tragic automobile accident while in college over twenty years ago), the Yoders have forty-two grandchildren and thirteen great-grandchildren.

Perhaps a measure of success in life could be indicated by home ownership, and each of my brothers and sisters has a home of his or her own. In fact, if one believes that parents aspire to have their children achieve a higher station in life than they have, then it's true to say that my parents' aspirations have been filled. Although only the

Internal Revenue Service knows for certain, I'm sure all of the brothers and sisters would agree that materially, we have all reached beyond our parents. We would also agree that we have a long way to go before we reach their accomplishments.

Many who have read portions or all of the previous pages have asked, "Where are the problems?" "How could this story unfold with such constant success?" "Aren't you glossing over the pain?" etc., etc. It is obviously legitimate to raise these questions. To argue that there were no moments of sadness or hardship would be inaccurate; but, in truth, such moments do pale before the happy times. As I've said a number of times, our parents knew how to manage. And, of course, we were fortunate. Devastating problems didn't visit our doorstep. Illnesses were of the common cold variety; problems were of the "low grade in chemistry" variety. The potential problems created by the international family were averted for the reasons related. Yes, it was a remarkable achievement.

The kinds of traps that seem possible were never really sprung. And the children, who could have been so destitute, considering the options available for them in their youth, grew and matured in a way that was truly marvelous. All my brothers and sisters recognize this and offer testimony of love and devotion to our parents. I hope with the telling of this story, readers will feel likewise.

Epilogue

Another holiday season is here. Last month, Thanksgiving required two full-sized turkeys to feed the thirty-nine family members who found their way to our mountain. It was a Thanksgiving feast with all the trimmings, brought in covered dishes by brothers, sisters, and offspring. Now, it is the Christmas season, and again, the family gathers to celebrate a special time.

As we settle in the family room of my sister's comfortable home, it is easy to feel the glowing warmth of the crackling fire, and the bountiful love so evident. The house is filled with excited voices. Some are the little children eager to get to the presents under the tree; others are older cousins swapping tales of school or friends; and, of course, my brothers and sisters share the memories of the old days—the mammoth Welcome House Christmas tree, the "colder winter," the "deeper snows," the "better times." Whenever such reminiscing takes place, there is always the presence of our parents and their continuing influence that all of us feel as we go about our daily lives.

As the family shares its joys and enthusiasm for the holidays, there is a sense of unity, a feeling of oneness. By contrast, it is sad and ironic to contemplate the many racial, religious, and political divisions of the world—Arab against Israeli in the Middle East, Protestant against Catholic in Northern Ireland, black against white in South Africa; black against white in New York City, ethnic divisions in what once was the Soviet Union, continuing tensions in the Balkans, and on and on and on. Can there be no end?

Perhaps a personal experience offers some glimmer of hope in response to my question. Some years ago I had the opportunity to lecture to a black group on a white man's view of the history of racism and prejudice in the United States. A long list of specific references to many horrors inflicted on Black Americans by the White Power structure aroused some expected and natural hostility among the listeners. The glares were obvious, the anger clearly felt. As we turned to a discussion period, a young black woman stood to speak, but her eyes were sad, not angry. In a soft voice she asked, "Are we all really so different? Why can't we love one another?"

I think of that young woman's inquiry now as I ponder the tragedy of a divided world torn by intolerance and prejudice, and then I look around this room during this happy Christmas season. Here there is a spirit of love and joy. Here there is a bond. And all this is shared by individuals who are so obviously from different worlds, but who just as obviously exist in a cohesive family unit. I answer now, just as I answered that young woman. "Why indeed? Why indeed?"